Memoirs of a Gambler

Philip M John

ISBN-13: 9798883766519

COVER DESIGN BY

ALICE HUNT

For Jean, Byron, Sarah, Jess, and Rocky.

CONTENTS

PREFACE

This book is a true, open, and honest account of my gambling journey. It spans an eight-year period, starting in the summer of 2014. It should be read chronologically, and there are some serious and extreme gambling themes which may not be suitable for all readers. I have purposely omitted detailed explanations of the rules of the card and casino games where they are not essential to the story. Some names and character descriptions have been fictionalised to protect identities. I hope my story not only serves as a warning but also provides hope.

1. AMSTERDAMNATION

Amsterdam was charming in the promising sunshine of July. World Cup fever was in full grip and the Dutch colours were draped like oranges from pillar to post. I was in Amsterdam to celebrate that I'd completed university, one of the first in my family ever to hold a degree. My friends and I were looking for postgraduate careers now, but before that we wanted to mark the end of an era with this trip.

I was eager to indulge in the delights that the Dutch capital was so famous for: historic museums, quaint canals, liberal red lights, and, perhaps, a particular type of cake that may not be lawfully obtained in the land of my fathers. However, it was a drug of a different kind that would shape my visit to the city... and the entire course of my life.

The summer sun was setting beautifully, its final rays shimmering across the city's canals. It was complemented by an almost chaotic freedom as the cyclists infested the streets and the vehicles seemed to flow instinctively through a maze of intersections and tramlines. It was much more liberal than my homeland and it all seemed to work, just about.

Within a few minutes of walking, we arrived at the casino. It was located in a charming little square of bars and restaurants with a water fountain as its centrepiece. Inside, it looked more like Las Vegas with its rich red carpets, flashing lights, immaculate staff, and not a clock in sight.

I had frequented the casinos of Cardiff in the past, never spending more than about forty pounds, but this felt a little different. Despite it seeming larger and, I suppose, more exclusive, we were not expecting a ten-euro charge to enter. I looked at Minty, the marginally shorter of my two compatriots, and he pulled his usual expression of slight dissatisfaction but reluctant acceptance.

We had all been fairly decided on our plan for the evening, so we paid up and headed straight for the bar. We took our Dutch beers and found ourselves an empty table. It was at this point that I noticed a specific signposted section of the casino exclusively for Texas hold 'em poker. I knew the others had no interest in the temptations of the house, so I encouraged them to go ahead to the restaurant should I not return within a suitable time frame. In truth, I didn't intend on playing for more than an hour. As it turned out, I did not end up taking any longer than this, but it was by no means the hour I was expecting…

"Excuse me, are there any tables opening up?" I enquired with one of the croupiers.

"Yes, sir. Please take a seat here." She directed me to an empty table. "Minimum buy-in is one hundred euros."

She informed me of that just as I was about to take forty euros out of my wallet.

I tried to maintain a sense of composure, but I was slightly shocked. I suppose it was my pride that stopped me from walking away at this point, and in my head I quickly formulated a plan to fold a few hands, finish my drink, and walk away without too much embarrassment.

The table instantly filled up, and there were nine players including myself. I can't say I took too much notice of the others but, after taking a nervous sip of my beer, it unsettled me when I saw them exchanging mountains of notes for stacks of one-hundred-euro chips.

I was going to start this game as the short stack by several hundred, and as I finally began to look into the eyes of my fellow players, I could see them staring at my pocket change. I took a large swig of my beer and looked across at the dealer, willing him to get it over with.

The dealer did not look much older than me, maybe twenty-five, but he was a competent professional and hypnotised us with an exotic dance with the cards before stopping them dead in the middle of the green-clothed table. He proceeded to spread them out face up across the table before collecting them again and placing them into the shuffling machine. The game was on.

Directly opposite me and to the immediate left of the dealer, there sat a black man wearing lightly tinted sunglasses who I would have guessed was in his mid-thirties – he looked very composed, so we'll refer to him simply as the Shark. He was sitting next to a slim, black-haired lady who was the only woman at the table. To my left was a bald, white European man. He was speaking what I assumed was Dutch to a dark-haired man to his left – I would later discover that they were both Danish.

The young dealer tossed the cards effortlessly, one at a time, to the nine players until we each had two cards. I nervously lifted the tips of my cards to reveal the nine of clubs and the four of hearts – a nothing hand that would be easy for me to fold, allowing me to relax and take a further sip of my beer.

A few forgettable hands passed in a similar fashion and my beer was almost empty – seemed like a good time to walk away without too much indignity after one more hand. One more hand.

I lifted the cards to see two red aces staring at me like a pair of hypnotic eyes, and they were bullets I could not let go unfired. I hoped to pick up a few extra chips before, and after, the first three community cards were dealt – five in total would eventually be dealt. To my pleasant surprise, the decision was soon made for me as, after the two Danes had folded, a middle-aged man with a full, thick, and greying beard raised one hundred euros – I'll refer to him as Captain Birdseye, and I sincerely hoped he would not catch the fish at this table. It was a huge bet in comparison to my own stack of chips, which was roughly eighty-five euros' worth. If I were to call, I would be all-in, and that was really all of the money I had been intending to spend on the rest of my travels.

I tried to maintain a calm exterior, but it proved even more difficult when the Shark raised a further one hundred euros and was subsequently called by the dark-haired woman next to him. I had little time to think as the next player folded and all eyes turned to face me for my decision. There was absolutely no question that I would play the hand. It was the jackpot hand: two (known as "pocket") aces, the best hand you can start with. But my hesitation came because of the stakes. At this point in time, it would be by far the biggest single bet I had ever made, and the biggest pot by some way.

"All-in," I announced with attempted conviction, though my heart was pounding as I tried my best to steady my hand whilst placing my chips in the centre of the table. A side-pot was to be played out with the remaining players as they still had chips to continue betting with, but all I could do was sit and watch, and hope, as the round played out.

A jack and a nine of spades with the two of diamonds – the first two cards were ominous as they presented several possibilities for hands that could all be superior to my pair of aces. Captain Birdseye raised a huge two hundred euros, and I was astonished at how casually he could toss the chips into the centre of the table and out of his grasp. It was also a worrying sign that he may have something in his hand worth significant investment – or, I wondered, was it a staggering bluff?

The Shark did not think for very long before

reluctantly sliding his cards face down towards the dealer, confirming his fold of the hand. The sole woman decided to call, at which point I saw Captain Birdseye noticeably stroking his buried jawline – was that a sign of weakness?

The dealer presented the fourth out of the five community cards: the six of hearts, which would surely have no real influence. Whatever that card meant for the players left in, it did not diminish the aggressive tactics of Captain Birdseye. He placed a further three hundred euros into the pot, which was more than the lady's stack. She was not deterred in the slightest, and without any comment, slid her remaining stack into the pot.

The players decided not to reveal their hands before the fifth and final community card was dealt. The final card was another six; this one was clubs. To my relief, it ruled out the possibility of a flush – five cards of the same suit.

"Sir…" The dealer gave me the nod as I was in the position required to reveal their hand first, so I cautiously placed my aces face up on the table. It attracted audible approval and a number of claps from the other players and those few spectators who had gathered around the table. I hadn't noticed them as I was so engrossed in the game.

Captain Birdseye was not impressed and revealed an ace and a jack. He'd bet extravagantly and faithfully with his one pair of jacks. The woman revealed that both of her cards were queens. Nothing that the dealer had presented gave them anything that could trump my aces, and I was about to receive over two hundred and fifty euros as my share of the bets. The lady would win the side-pot that had built up between her and Captain Birdseye, which was also quite a sum!

I was overjoyed with the win and decided another beer was in order. I planned to indulge in a few more rounds of betting and then head off to treat my fellow travellers to a few more beverages than we had originally anticipated.

"A great time to have the aces," said the bald man in very good English with a mild Scandinavian accent.

"I certainly can't complain," I replied through a beaming smile.

I threw a few bets in here and there to speculate, to which the other players responded by folding. My stack suddenly appeared in far greater health than when I had first taken my seat.

I continued the friendly conversation with the bald man, who introduced himself as Karl. He was Danish and had been working in Amsterdam for a few days. He was generally more accustomed to a game of blackjack and only occasionally frequented the poker tables. I gathered that the table had more of his ilk – wealthy men and women from the world of business and commerce. And then, of course, there was me, a self-unemployed graduate from the post-mining, working-class valleys of south Wales. On this night, however, I was enjoying the novelty of going head-to-head with the high rollers. My good fortune may have earned me a bit more respect around the table, and I was more relaxed about being involved. The second beer was like golden nectar trickling with the joy of my good luck.

I was at the table for less than an hour, but it still felt like an all-night affair. A nine and ten of clubs found their way to me and I told myself that it would be the last hand. I should return to my friends, who would soon be leaving the bright lights behind for an evening meal. A relaxed, small succession of bets encouraged me to stay in the hand to see what the young dealer would conjure up for my swansong.

The jack, the queen, and the four of clubs were revealed... a flush, five cards of the same suit, right from the off. I could have punched the air with delight. As that might just have given the game away, I calmly placed thirty euros into the pot. To my disbelief, the Shark pushed all of his chips into the centre – he was all in. With that, another player, a young, blond-haired man who a waiter had referred to as Rudy, matched the bet. My heart rate rose considerably once again, and though I tried my best not to show any emotion, I have no doubt that my face was beginning to show signs of excitement.

I could not let this one go. I called the bet and placed my sum of just over three hundred euros into the pot. I rarely had that sort of money in my bank account at any one time, let alone to hand over in one single bet. I had never really considered myself to be a serious gambler and I felt like things were unfolding outside of my control. I was yet to experience the flipside of such sensations, but I was fully intending to ride the waves of fortune whilst they were going my way.

The dealer presented the king of hearts and the two

of diamonds to round off the game. Rudy turned over a king and a queen of spades, and as a consequence the Shark threw his cards to the dealer, face down, in disgust. I showed my flush and Rudy shouted something in Dutch – I can't imagine it was anything pleasant. The rest of the table and the several spectators gave another, louder round of applause. The dealer began to stack up my winnings as I stared, wide eyed, at the piles of chips in front of me.

"Not a bad evening for you, my friend." Karl congratulated me with a wry smile as I started to do a rough calculation. The adrenaline was running too high to work out the exact sum, but I knew it was over one thousand euros. I felt absolutely elated and, after the initial shock, I could not stop myself grinning from ear to ear. I'd never had a win that compared to this in the past – I'd never had the money to even consider betting enough, nor the desire to.

The dealer congratulated me and passed on my chips. Rudy had already left the table before the next hand was dealt. I folded a few more rounds whilst finishing another beer, wished Karl all the best, and thanked the dealer for his service before gathering my chips, ready to cash in.

I could not resist spreading my good news, and despite only having had a few beers, I felt as though I was on another planet and in some kind of utopia. My friends already knew – the expression on my face told them almost everything.

"Come on then, how much?"

I placed the chips on their table. "There's over a

thousand euros there, about nine hundred or so of profit."

I still could not stop smiling. It would definitely be a trip to remember.

I would love to say we celebrated in style in some classy bars and sought out some lively music venues, but on our second day we had a none-too-pleasant experience with a local bakery selling some rather interesting kinds of cakes.

I would be sharing the story of my wonderful stroke of luck upon my return and probably for some time to come. It's only when reflecting on my journey that this moment becomes so much more significant. Although it was a success story, much like the first story of many gamblers, it was also the very first time I experienced the dangerous side-effects of the gambling drug: the feeling of invincibility, the frenzied ecstasy of the win regardless of the consequences on the psyche, and a taste of gambling as a very fast, easy problem-solver. It was my first taste of the many different gambling flavours that I would become quite the connoisseur of in the years to follow.

2. OVER THE BRIDGE

The post-mining communities and villages of the Welsh Valleys had been decimated by a mass extraction of wealth from the industry, and then left for the rot to set in. The quaint, beautiful, and historic buildings were left to crumble along with the community, the language, and the culture, and I had to find a way to make sense of it all.

Those who grow up in this small corner of the world find it very painful to leave behind. Despite the challenges, the place becomes part of you, and you part of it. The deprivation throughout the Rhondda Valleys brought with it another kind of privilege – to have grown up with rolling hills either side of the terraced streets, where the imagination could run as wild as the streams and rivers, and a child could be enchanted by the wonder of the woods. The black of the coal mining collieries had long since been retired, and despite all the forgotten council estates, the green of my valley had returned in all its natural glory.

The warm celebrations of that summer, including my graduation, had been a time of great promise for me. There should have been an open highway of possibilities stretching into the near future and beyond. However, as the season began to fall, the summer's promise seemed to fade with the green of the leaves. I was having no luck in finding a suitable career, and as a young adult in one of these post-mining valleys, the opportunities were very slim. My studies had been focused on policing and criminology, and as a result of the economic recession, recruitment in those areas had ground to halt. I had no choice but to continue my services as a postgraduate painter and decorator.

"I bet you wished you went to school now, dun ew?!" exclaimed a baritone voice from just behind me.

I turned around to face a large, middle-aged plumber who had momentarily been observing me sanding away at some skirting boards. A coffee-stained smile emerged across his face as he followed up his comment with a loud, hearty laugh. I could not bring myself to say anything and just smiled and breathed out a very slight, forced chuckle. I was not quite so amused at hearing these words mere weeks after graduating with honours from university. It was not that I did not value learning a trade, nor did I have any problem putting in a hard day's graft, but I didn't feel like it was the best use of my strengths. The old plumber's sentiment became the motivation I needed to prove him wrong and make my way in the world.

The winter was really setting in, and I tried to fight off the feelings of despair about the lack of suitable job opportunities as I rolled paint onto the ceiling in one of the many houses on a newly built housing estate. My phone vibrated and I quickly dropped my roller with a glimmer of hope for a positive response from one of my recent job applications. Instead, it was the news that my maternal grandmother had passed away earlier that morning. Though she had been ill for some time, the sense of loss and distant memories flooded my thoughts. I continued my work in a sombre mood and soon returned home to my family.

My late grandmother was graced with a pleasant send-off, but it was not her dying days that really sprang to mind as I sat in the crematorium for the funeral service; rather, a pensive contemplation of the wonderful person that she was throughout her life. I thought of afternoons inside her old terraced home, stories of a working-class life in the colliery canteen serving the miners, as well as the years she spent running a corner shop. The experience and stories of these colourful, hard-working people will always be part of who I am – something that the very small percentage of society's inherently wealthy and greedy will never really have or understand. Did I really want to leave all of this behind?

This is exactly why it is so hard to leave. The geographical immobility is both financial and emotional. My home, my community, which had been through so much and left with nothing – how could I leave behind a place that had already been left behind? Although it would not be easy, I had to find a way to accept this, at least for now, and set my mind on finding better opportunities.

I was in regular contact with my sister, who had taken flight from the Welsh hills some years before to find work in the city of Bristol, and so I conducted my search for work further afield. An opportunity finally presented itself in the form of a trainee role within the procurement section of a government department. By late February, I was gathering up my worldly possessions and cramming them like a misfit of jigsaw pieces into my humble little automobile. It would be required to utilise the whole one litre of its engine on my journey across the Welsh border and over the Severn Bridge to a new life in Bristol.

The first few months of independence were perhaps more challenging than I had anticipated, and I questioned my capability and my own sense of purpose. I suddenly found myself sharing a house with several strangers, and the low wage I had accepted for this new chapter limited my options for the foreseeable future. The idea of packing up my things and heading back to my homeland to think again became more and more tempting. However, somewhere inside the chambers of my head and my heart, I knew that the lack of familiarity and feelings of discomfort were an essential part of the journey.

Bristol comes with its own unique charm, and the cobbled lanes aside the quaint waterways hold faint whispers of the traders and fishermen who had once been commonplace. Not only rich in history, the city was alive with diverse music in every other street, and environmental movements and initiatives were commonplace. I quickly began to feel the essence of the city, which helped to settle the sense of displacement.

During these first few months, I agreed to join my housemates for some farewell celebrations after one of them announced they were moving out and on to pastures new. We took the usual half-an-hour bus route to the city centre and discovered a very talented blues band in a quirky live music venue where we indulged in unacceptable amounts of spirits and beer.

Although my wages were very low in comparison with the cost of living in the city, I had no real regard for the material things in life. Yet I could not help but feel I was being wasteful of the little money I was bringing in, and during our taxi ride back to our accommodation, I could not stop my drunken mind from searching for a possible solution. The ecstatic memories of the evening of poker in Amsterdam washed over me like a hot shower on a cold winter morning. I already had an online betting account which I'd set up for the odd football accumulator or annual horse racing bet, but I was also aware of the plentiful variety of casino games available.

In my state of drunken insensibility, a conversation from a few days before with a colleague came to the forefront of my mind. They had told me of a roulette success story involving big bets on the short odds. A man who had risked thousands on a spin of the wheel and doubled his fortune in a matter of seconds. Off the back of that blurred memory, I conjured up a seemingly infallible plan of simply betting until I had restored all of the money I'd spent that evening, and what better, quicker way of doing so was there than the European roulette wheel? I switched on my computer with the intention of adding another zero onto my stake of ten pounds.

The black and red wheel was spinning ominously on my computer screen as I placed all ten pounds onto black. Following a click of the "spin" button, the small silver ball burst into life and began its slow, swirling descent towards the coloured numbers… Round and round it spun…

… Number 1, RED.

I gave an angry mutter at the thought of the ten pounds that had just gone in an instant, deleted from the screen as if it had never been in existence. I took a deep breath and deposited a further twenty pounds into the account. I would put the twenty pounds on the even numbers, bet, and then, regardless of the result, I would say goodnight. I wouldn't…

One more spin… *One more spin*…

… Number 25, ODD.

I shook my head in disappointment, but instead of angrily retiring to my bed, the competitive side of me came out in force. There was only so long the numbers could go against me, and I wasn't going to lose that night.

I've always been a fairly headstrong individual, rarely swayed by widespread opinions or popular culture, and

I was generally quite disciplined with my own physical health. However, regardless of how immune you believe yourself to be, you can very, very quickly lose yourself in the intensity of a gambling experience. The grip of the moment can be so hypnotic that it can be as devastating as a mind-altering drug. Another difficulty with self-restraint is the fact that gambling does not directly involve physical harm. Add drunkenness to the mix to further fuel a deadly fire.

... I would not let it go, and I deposited a further one hundred pounds... yes... that would put everything right and I could go to sleep a happy man. The whole one hundred pounds was placed on red...

... Number 24, BLACK.

I was beginning to feel sick, but I was entirely convinced that just by the law of averages I would soon be back to my winning ways. The thrill of the chase and a few small (large) drinks had reassured me of that fallacy. I poured myself a glass of water before proceeding to place a two-hundred-pound bet, followed by five hundred pounds. Yes, five hundred pounds, a sum of money that should have meant so very much to a man in my position in life.

I did not care much for the essence and concept of money, and combined with the total detachment that came with numbers appearing on the screen, I was like an inebriated lamb to the slaughter. The five hundred pounds was a losing bet, resulting in my loss of five consecutive even money bets. Whilst this is relatively unlucky in terms of odds, the odds are always stacked in the favour of the house and so consecutive losses are not actually that uncommon.

I had, for the first time, just experienced the dreaded losing streak (the losing streak is, of course, another myth, and, in fact, each round of betting is a brand new game). The following morning would bring with it more than a sore head for my overindulgence.

3. THE OLD TOWN

The biting cold of the following February only added to the untouchable mystique of one of the most beautiful European cities I have ever had the pleasure of exploring: Prague. With my somewhat minimalist attitude to life and my frugal approach to most monetary affairs following the gambling mishap the previous year, I had been able to ensure a reunion with my old friends for another misadventure.

We strolled in the direction of Charles Bridge without a care in the world. The modern quarter of the city had its fair share of shopping centres, tower blocks, and some very persistent men handing out leaflets in an attempt to recruit customers to the renowned adult entertainment clubs, colloquially known as "Titty Bars". I can't think why.

After fighting our way through the ticket sellers and the busy streets, I noticed a sign jutting out of a high-rise bar with a casino on the top floor. That warm glow of promise spiralled through me once again as I recalled the feeling of ecstasy after the remarkable poker win in Amsterdam. It could have been the perfect way to rectify my night of inebriated nonsense at the online roulette wheel and relive the successes of that night just two years earlier.

The existence of the bar within the casino was enough bargaining power to convince my friends to join me whilst I graced the tables. Although the ground-floor bar area was fairly modern with its new blue carpet and recently painted walls of red and gold, the place was markedly different from the previous casinos I'd visited. As we made our way up the stairs to the main floor of the casino, we arrived inside a smoke-filled, dimly lit room of green tables. It felt like we had travelled at least fifty years into the past, and I began to doubt my seemingly bright idea of reliving past triumph.

As my companions faded into the shadows and made their way across the far end of the room to the gambling machines, I sat myself at an unwelcoming table of around six Texas hold 'em players and placed my 1500 Czech crowns (the equivalent of about fifty British pounds) onto the table and pushed them towards the dealer.

Thankfully, the minimum buy-in was slightly less than the extravagant table I had played at in Amsterdam. I was eyed sternly by an ageing, long-haired man of East Asian descent who was puffing pensively on his cigarette. The dealer presented me with my stack of chips and quickly dealt the first hand of the evening. The eyes of the jack of diamonds staring back at me were accompanied by the two of spades, and so I folded my hand without much further thought.

Several hands went by with not much to show for them, and my patience was waning so much that I decided to take a punt on a mediocre hand – a queen and a nine of hearts. The dealer presented the first three community cards as the four and five of hearts and the king of spades. One more heart and I would have myself a queen-high flush.

The long-haired old man raised aggressively by two hundred Czech crowns (about seven British pounds) and three players folded like dominoes until the buck stopped with me. I looked again at the two hearts already on the table and stared into the eyes of my long-haired opponent. He just had to be hiding a big grin behind the emotionless mask. Yes, he most definitely had something worth betting for, and the odds of me finding another heart in the next two cards to be dealt were around four-to-one. It would have made more sense to fold, but I'd become restless and impatient. Lack of patience is a big factor in the downfall of a gambler. It was unusual for me, but the unsavoury environment had got the better of me.

"Raise three hundred," I announced, hoping that I would be understood by the dealer at least.

The old man called without a second's thought and the dealer swiftly revealed the next card – the ten of diamonds. Seemingly irrelevant, yet the man raised by a further three hundred. That was the time to fold; my odds of a flush had reduced significantly and I'd have simply been hoping for the last card to pay off. Unfortunately, my impatience had consumed me, and not only did I call the raise of three hundred, but I raised a further four hundred Czech crowns, which was the last of my remaining chips… All in.

The man very briefly looked at his cards and part of me clung on to the hope that he was considering the fold. He proceeded to place a handful of chips in the centre of the table and gave a slight nod toward the dealer to signify his call. All my chances of salvation rested on a heart.

Neither of us revealed our cards in advance of the dealer placing the fifth and final community card on display. It was the ten of spades. And it was the spade that dug the grave of my flush that wasn't to be. It was on the old man to reveal his hand first, but I already knew that I had lost. He confirmed the forgone conclusion with his two kings, making a full house with the king and pair of tens already on the table. A strong hand played well, although the reserved size of his early betting could have backfired if my heart had shown itself and the final king had failed to appear.

The dealer looked at me in anticipation of any further buy-in, and I politely declined by standing up to leave the table. I decided to retain some professional integrity by offering a hand to the better man, which he reciprocated and for the first time displayed something that resembled a smile – I wasn't surprised, with the stack of chips heading in his direction. I needed to get out of the smoke box and find myself something stronger to drink to wash away the pain of the failed attempt to rekindle former glory – an endless and futile pursuit for many a gambler.

Later that same evening, I found myself very much in my element in the dimly lit corner of the Agharta Jazz Club with some Czech ale, good company, and fine musicians. On the way to the venue, we had seen the sign swinging in a gentle breeze outside the unassuming location in the side streets of the Old Town. The stairs led down into a 14th-century basement setting. It was as if the old walls spoke the language of the past and were the perfect entrance to the pensive, moody, and beautiful jazz performance. We took up our table, and the saxophone players worked their magic as we sat back and drank. And drank some more. The applause was aplenty and so were the ales, the gins, the cocktails... by which point we were ready for the stumble home.

On the way back towards the entrance, several very strong nightcaps were ordered, and as my friends were knocking them back, I caught sight of the band members sitting on the far edge of the bar. In my very merry state, I could not pass up the chance to offer my thanks and praise for the wonderful show. I began to tell them of my homeland and how it would be such a pleasure to see them perform live there. A local Czech gentleman joined our conversation with the musicians and had noticed how we were indulging in much of the top row of the bar. He ordered several shots of a Czech liquor that he spoke very highly of. I'm sure it would have been wonderful had we not had far too much already, but it proved to be the fatal blow to our visit to the Old Town.

The exit from the jazz bar that evening was a

complete blur, but I do remember flashes of our drunken stumble back to the apartment because we sang at the top of our voices – only the following morning did we realise that street singing in the capital was banned during those hours. But something I do remember was a moment of temptation. As we came within sight of the apartment, the poker loss came back from the recesses of my blurred mind, and I thought again about the roulette wheel, and righting my wrongs. It was my last thought before crashing into a drunken slumber. The deadly combination of alcohol and gambling had not quite coincided… this time.

4. THE BASEMENT

Life was cruising with many open roads up ahead. A promotion was on the horizon, and I was contemplating where I should pledge my future and the next phase of my life. Though I had learned from some of my mistakes along the way, I was still very much lost in the malaise of my early twenties. I felt as though I had lost part of myself by leaving behind my home and all of those dying communities – was a part of myself dying in the process? I still belonged to my home, but that wasn't enough to stop me searching for another purpose, not just in my own life but in the world around me.

I had moved to another department since the previous summer, but I received an invitation from the colleagues I had worked with when I first joined the organisation, asking me along to a social gathering in the city centre. I casually accepted without any real consideration about whether or not I would actually make an appearance.

It was Friday evening and I sat amongst my housemates with a cold beer, relaxing in our shared lounge as the night slowly blackened the view of our small garden. Some of my housemates offered to join me in the city for some light ales. I was still uncertain if I was really feeling up to it after a long week, and with a promotion application to be working on, I was hoping to be at my freshest the following morning.

I received a message from Jess, a young lady I was introduced to on my very first day, asking if I would be attending and that they were at the first pub. We hadn't been in touch since I changed department, and I responded neutrally with a further question about how long they would be there, still undecided about whether I was going. I don't quite know if it was because I had the option of my housemates' company for the bus journey or whether the cold beer was some encouragement, but I sensed that it would do no harm to show my face even if it was just for a couple.

A couple indeed.

Several beers and cocktails on and we found ourselves in a nightclub playing an eclectic mix of songs from the decades gone by. I can't say I remember spending more of the evening with Jess than with anyone else, but a middle-aged lady who was part of the group approached me.

"So what about you and Jess?" she enquired abruptly.

"Sorry? What do you mean?"

"Oh I'm sure there's something there, isn't there?" she said semi-convincingly through a wry smile.

I laughed along without much to say, as it wasn't something I had really considered. There's no doubt that it had been a pleasure to work with an attractive young lady of a similar age, but I had always been quite professional in that sense, and there had not been any follow-up contact of any kind. But a spark had now been lit by this small suggestion and a few light ales.

The music, and the drinks, continued late into the evening, and in the hazy film reel in my memory there was a breathtakingly romantic dance followed by a warm embrace and the first of many kisses. In reality, there was a drunken fumbling ritual that I'm sure would have made an impressive nature documentary. However it looked, it was the beginning of some very good times, leaving the gambling mistake – and, for that matter, any other mistake – firmly in yesterday's scrapbook.

In the months that followed my reunion with Jess, we stayed in regular contact and frequented many eateries, bars, and restaurants in and around Bristol. It was very much like spending time with an old friend whom I had known for many years. There can often be cultural and political barriers for people from my working-class walk of life, but Jess came from a solid, hard-working family, which only added to our compatibility. I've always been a bit of an old-fashioned gentleman, despite my relatively younger age, so it seemed quite fitting that our relationship blossomed in quite an old-fashioned way. So, for all of my gambling experiences past and present, it will always be this unexpected companionship that was my greatest stroke of luck.

I was planning to take Jess back to Wales and into the floating hills of home to meet the vibrant array of characters that were my family and friends, including my father's mother. Although my hometown was full of fantastical Welsh characters, my Nanny John (as she was colloquially known) had joined the valley during World War II from the Emerald Isle across the Irish Sea. It is with much sadness that I was never able to take Jess to meet her, as I spent many weekends travelling back alone to the hospital to visit her with my close family. At the age of ninety-three, she had, as she would so often say, "passed her sell-by date" and after a few weeks of illness, she passed on peacefully in hospital.

It was a poignant moment when I was given the news, but rather than just feeling deeply saddened, I simultaneously felt an energy and a sense of purpose. I made a decision not to shut away these deep, meaningful emotions in the basement, but instead to channel them into some sort of tribute. The life of my grandmother and her character came to me in the form of words. They sang to me of all the good times and all I had learned. What struck me the most was that, for her to have had such an impact on me in my two decades or so of life, her impact in her ninety-three years on Earth must surely be something to write about!

I think all of us have a basement. A place we keep under lock and key, deep down inside the heart and the mind. The things we choose to put inside this place of ours are a range of our own experiences, regrets, fears, trauma, sadness, grief, anger, and all of those trials and tribulations in our lives. And life in modern times can race ahead at such a pace that we force ourselves to keep these experiences (or demons) secured firmly in our basements. The problem is that there is only so much room in our basement, and when the monsters break free they can cause absolute devastation, not only by consuming us but by destroying those closest to us. I have come to realise the importance of opening the door to this basement from time to time, harnessing the energy inside, and ultimately taming the demons into a positive force. Sometimes it can be difficult to realise the importance of this. In my foolish naivety, I used gambling as a mechanism to deal with a full basement instead of openly discussing it and facing up to it. However, this time I could take solace from the fact that I opened the basement and faced up to things in a more positive, and less self-destructive, way.

I was inspired and scribbled some rhyming couplets down on a notepad. It had been some time since I had explored my creativity and affinity with writing and poetry, but I conjured up these feelings and the energy from somewhere deep down inside. From the basement. After sharing it with close family members, they kindly requested for it to be part of the funeral readings, and although I know it was not expected of me, I nonetheless felt a sense of duty to perform the reading of my poem.

The summer rain had been relentless in the week that followed the death of my grandmother, but on the morning of the funeral, the sun came out for the send-off. It sat gloriously in the sky in contrast to the sombre mood of friends and family alike. Some biblical readings were made before my summons to step up to the altar. My duty had also helped to channel my energy and so I was feeling focused on the day, albeit a little nervous. I introduced myself and cleared my throat before reading the few verses that I can only hope went some way to giving a deserved send-off...

Here's a few words I thought I'd put together,
Just to say why it's Nanny John I'll remember forever.

As she would say it,
She was "as strong as an ox, as fit as a flea...
Billy Whizz, that's what they would call me!"
Setting sail from Ireland to see what life could be
With heart, courage and a nice cup of tea.

Working hard as a nurse in Leicester,
What else in life would be next to test her?
It brought her to Wales but that's not such a mystery,
She fell in love with a soldier and the rest is history.

Her family began but her loved one suddenly passed,
Six young children, an impossible task.
She used her strength and took on the test,
Whatever life dealt she gave it her very best.

The generosity was endless, no kindness was a chore
Her family was her life, it's everything she lived for.

The last few years were not so easy,
She struggled on, still strong and steely.

But after all this time she hadn't lost her spark,
She loved us all right from the start.

Full of knowledge and wise old phrases,
Talk of old times and Irish places,
Her joy and her laughter I will always miss,
What I'd give now for one more "God Bless" and a goodnight kiss.

A head full of wisdom and a heart of gold,
I thought you'd be here forever even at 93 years old.
Even though I'm sad,
I know you're at peace and for that I'm glad,
So "wash your hands" and "put the kettle on",
How blessed we all are to have had you, Nanny John.

5. BACK AT THE WHEEL

On an unassuming Sunday afternoon in early spring, I was talking to a work colleague about gambling, specifically roulette. We spoke about the stacked odds and how tactics are used to try to find a way around this in an attempt to make a profit – all of which are flawed in their own different ways. Nonetheless, it got me thinking, and as you might expect, my horrible loss the previous year had not been sitting well in my memory bank. Other than one moment of madness the previous winter, I had not approached roulette very often nor with any real conviction, but this conversation lit the spark of a dormant explosive within my brain which I just couldn't seem to ignore.

We talked about a very dangerous set of tactics known as the martingale – a range of betting strategies that in its simplest form involves doubling the stake after a loss. The fundamental problem with this is that whilst the odds will eventually fall in your favour and recoup any losses, you will never have an infinite amount of wealth or stake money and a streak of losing bets can so very easily result in bankruptcy. It is truly frightening to experience how quickly this strategy can get out of hand, particularly for someone who is not from a very wealthy walk of life.

I was not really interested in the money itself, nor was I much of a tactical gambling guru, but something told me that I could use this tool to recoup and recover from my terrible mistake. Thanks to my competitive spirit and my unwavering determination to right my wrongs, I would embark on a treacherous path: taking on the house.

I opened my laptop in the living room of my shared accommodation with the intention of playing online using the same account as that dreadful evening the previous year. I deposited ten pounds into the account but, this time, I wouldn't just place bets on red or black, or odd or even. I would spread the odds to increase the probability of a win and therefore place two simultaneous bets on the dozens and the columns.

The dozens represent the numbers 1–12, 13–24, and 25–36; the columns are the vertical sets of twelve numbers, which are also separated into three sections similarly to the dozens. The zero factor ultimately results in the odds being stacked in favour of the house. There are thirty-seven segments, the zero and 1–36, on the roulette wheel, with odds of 35–1 when betting on any individual number, which gives an edge of over two percent to the house. However, my mission was to significantly increase my odds by betting on two sets of twelve numbers. Fortune can favour the brave on some occasions, and repeated wins can result in a significant gain. But this tantalising possibility also brings with it the omnipresent risk of catastrophic loss.

I had not for a second contemplated another catastrophe, particularly as I had deposited just ten pounds (yet this is all it takes – a gateway drug). Starting with five pounds placed upon the first dozen (1–12) and the other five pounds placed upon the third dozen (25–36), I gave the go ahead with the click of a button and that tiny ball jumped into life once again. The feeling returned instantly – a tumultuous combination of excitement and dread.

The ball landed on a number in the second dozen, resulting in a ten-pound loss. I reminded myself of the patience required with this technique and proceeded to place another ten pounds on the first dozen. To mix things up, I placed a further ten pounds on the second dozen. Lo and behold, the number 23 came out for the second time in a row. The money (in this case, ten pounds) placed on the first dozen would be lost and taken by the house, but the ten pounds I had placed upon the second twelve would be paid out at the odds of 2–1, resulting in a thirty-pound return.

The relatively small win proved to be the catalyst in my chaotic relationship with the roulette wheel. I decided to divide my thirty pounds equally on the first and second columns (fifteen pounds on each column). The virtual ball fumbled into the slot marked number 16 – the first column – resulting in a return of thirty pounds in addition to the return of fifteen pounds of my stake money. The fifteen placed on the second column would be sacrificed to the house.

And so it went on for the best part of half an hour. I continued to place split bets on the 2–1 odds, with the odd setback, but I decided to draw the line at £310. That was quite a return for half an hour's work, and I was stunned not only at how easy it was but how so very rapidly the situation can change. The extreme yo-yoing of emotions was incredibly damaging, but even in my self-proclaimed maturity and with my inner voice of reason, I failed to recognise just how harmful it was and would continue to be. I distinctly remember sharing news of my impressive flutter at the wheel with some of my family back in Wales. Little did anyone know about my sizeable loss the previous year, nor did they know just how far the journey would go. For that matter, neither did I.

Three days later, the warm feeling had not subsided, and there was almost a nagging sense of unfinished business that played on my mind in the few days that followed. Later that same week I decided that, following my win, I had nothing to lose by testing the mettle of the winning streak to right the wrongs of the previous year once and for all.

This philosophy is one that has plagued many gamblers throughout history – the will to put things right, to win back the losses and retire happily into the sunset. The powerful pull of this fallacy is comparable to the dark voices within the mind of those addicted to substances – "one more hit" becomes "one more bet". The martingale strategy hinges on this mindset and the variations of this ideology set me on my catastrophically damaging gambling journey.

My eyes were transfixed once more by the spinning of reds, blacks, and a solitary green square for the zero – the house's edge. My win had restored some of my betting confidence, and I was then placing twenty pounds on two sets of columns, along with two sets of twenty pounds across the blocks of twelve numbers. It was a total bet of eighty pounds, which was again creeping into the territory of my Amsterdam experience in terms of total value per bet. I had very few losses over the course of seven or eight bets, and before I knew it, the £300 I had earned the previous weekend had become just shy of £800. I was ecstatic to have almost recouped the entirety of my overall losses.

I didn't have any real interest in or obsession with the material value of the money I was betting with – it was the competitive spirit willing me to get even. And as soon as I'd recouped my losses, which I was wholeheartedly convinced I would, I could put this all behind me and carry on about my business.

I made two more bets that evening whereby I slightly changed my approach in hope of racing to the finish line. I placed a fifty-pound stake on black and a further fifty on evens – I was back in the same territory of the drunken malaise that occurred just twelve months earlier. If that bet were to come in, it would be £100 of profit and I would be within arm's reach of breaking even overall.

But it didn't. The bet was lost. Time to stop.

Although my ability to stop at this point may show self-discipline and strength of character, it was also conducted in a moment of sobriety.

What is startling about all of it, on reflection, is the total disconnect I experienced due to the click of a button and the lack of physical transaction. No physical, tangible exchange had been made between myself and the betting company, but rather some numbers were floating across the screen from one account to another, and eventually would be sucked into the vortex of the dark underbelly of the capitalist dream.

6. ONE MORE BET

I still perceived myself to be the controller of my own destiny. I had a slick win on the poker tables of Europe to my name and I had bitten back against the house for exploiting a moment of vulnerable drunkenness. Yet, I felt so deflated in the fortnight after that successful run of hearty victories at the Devil's Wheel (the suitable pseudonym for European roulette). I put it down to the fact that I hadn't quite come full circle. Not quite rounded things off exactly at the break-even point. Yes, I would only tame my restless thoughts when this was achieved.

Here you can draw a poignant comparison to drug addiction. Regardless of whether the addict is winning or losing, the elation, the grip, the hook, and the pull of the hit – in this case a bet – is one that cannot be replaced by the dreary and mundane pace of everyday life. This is difficult to truly understand without the experience of it: the comedown after the roller coaster ride of the gambling experience and the inability to readjust to normality. Betting with five, ten, even twenty-pound stakes suddenly seems underwhelming and worthless. What is most dangerous about this perception is that it does not reflect reality. In its tangible form, I still see the value of this money as I have never been a wealthy man, in the sense of capital. But in the world of online gambling, I was becoming more and more detached from reality.

The fading light of the March sunshine could scarcely be seen in the garden of my shared accommodation in the northern suburbs of Bristol. The month marked my second year since leaving the Welsh Valleys for a new life in the city, but I was not reflecting on my journey to date nor the real richness I had already won – self-sufficiency, horizons broadened by people and place, and, most importantly, finding my soulmate. No, I gave it not a second's thought, as I had already committed to signing my soul over to the Devil's Wheel.

There I was again, convincing myself that I was a whisker away from wiping the slate clean and walking away untarnished by the horrible world of greedy gambling companies and their vulnerable victims. There I was, someone apparently immune from such tragic frailties, falling prey to the vultures of capitalism. Gamblers are often vilified and looked upon as a disgrace, but gambling is comparable to any other addiction, yet one that seems so available, so well-marketed, with so few protections, such little awareness, and so much more that could be done to support those recovering.

I was no longer in the territory of the previous month, or any of my previous experiences. I had won several hundred and so I convinced myself that I could utilise recent gains without guilt. Without my careful, informed, and reasoned betting techniques, none of that money would have existed – another terrible mindset which would haunt me.

I placed fifty pounds on the first twelve, and fifty pounds on the second twelve, which is a significant amount of money for a single bet for a man in my circumstances, or so you would think, but I genuinely believed that it was a warmup. My mindset had already progressed to an irreversible stage in my gambling journey. That little silver ball dribbled into the tray of number 14 of the roulette wheel. "YES!" I exclaimed in an empty room, with the only noise coming from the television in the open-plan kitchen and lounge area of my shared accommodation. I was unaware as to whether any of my housemates were around, but if they were, they had either made themselves scarce or had simply not heard.

I repeated the same bet to no avail, and to my dismay the number 34 resulted in a fifty-pound loss due to the hundred-pound stake required to place this kind of bet. The problem was surfacing again just like it had done in Prague – impatience. I wanted out of it as soon as possible. Not only did I want to draw a line in the sand, but the feeling of the loss was truly sickening. Even though I was losing my grasp on the value of the money I was betting with, the ball of anger, resentment, and defiance when faced with a losing bet was just too much to take.

I placed one hundred pounds on the first of the three column sections, and a further hundred on the second column. It covered over sixty-five percent of the roulette table. This time, it was enough. Although one of the columns would always lose, the winning column returned at 2–1. The silver ball landed firmly in the trap of the number 1, and £300 was returned to my account.

That proved to be the beginning of a very special evening. I repeated three bets of a similar nature and they all won. I restored the majority of my losses and recaptured the glory of the evening at the poker tables of Amsterdam. What a perfect moment it would have been to walk away.

The explanation of why this is always a harder step to take than many might believe rests with the fundamental concept that any money that has been won cannot be lost. So, if a gambler wins several thousands of pounds worth of profit, they may then bet with this money with complete freedom. The paradoxical nature of this money that has been won is that, without the gambling activity, it would not have existed in the first place. It is such a dangerous idea, one that can break your spirit.

I was completely absorbed in this world. Consumed. Despite being able to apply self-discipline fairly well in most endeavours, other than the odd alcohol-fuelled hiccup, I was unable to recognise my own vulnerability. The difficulty for me was that gambling did not inflict any physical harm but was really an attack on mental health and the psyche. Sometimes, this can be a lot harder to recognise and accept.

I proceeded to begin doubling my stake up to £200 on each set of twelve, resulting in a total of £400 per bet. It was unfathomable. Money that would have been worth so very much to me. Money I was supposed to be saving to help me with making my way in life and establishing myself in the modern world. I was completely detached from reality. I was plugged into a toxic system that I had foolishly convinced myself I was in full control of.

I alternated my tactics between betting on two sets of twelve to betting on black or red as well as odd or even. My losses were very intermittent, and within the space of two more hours, I was in a profit of over £2,000. Before the night was over, I decided to have "one more bet". I had stepped over the boundary, and there would be no going back. A gambler who has been exposed to this level of betting can take a significant amount of time to be able to revert to betting at lower levels, at more reasonable amounts. In fact, much like many long-term, suffering alcoholics, moderation may never again be possible.

The "final" bet was, by this point, the most money I had placed on any single bet, and it exceeded even that of my Amsterdam casino poker evening three years prior. Like a man possessed, I placed £200 on red, £200 on odd, £200 on the first set of twelve (1–12) and £200 on the third set of 12 (25–36) – a total stake of £800. My eyes were wired and staring like a rabid predator at the spinning wheel on the computer screen. The irony is that I was, and always had been, the prey. Round and round the metal ball spun, with my fate hanging on a single moment. After three stuttering bounces it finally fell into place on the number 29, black. Although I had lost both the £200 placed upon red and the standard sacrifice of the stake on one of the sets of twelve, I had a £400 return on the bet placed on odd, and a £600 return from the bet placed on the third set of twelve. It was a £1,000 return from a single bet. I was actually shaking with a combination of adrenaline, shock, thrill, and disbelief. I was now well over £3,000 in profit and I was completely lost in the moment. I closed my laptop with absolutely no idea of what was to follow in the coming weeks.

7. THE BIG WIN

I did not widely broadcast my roulette activity aside from an occasional update to Jess and a mention of reasonably good fortune to family and friends. I failed to recognise it as the development of an obsession, and there had barely been time for reflection.

Two days after my incredible run of luck and I was about to do battle with the Devil and his wheel once again. I was beginning to fool myself that my betting methods had something to do with the miraculous win. The gambling site I was using did not process withdrawal payments until three working days had passed, which added further detachment from the true value of the money I'd won.

Spring was beginning to work its magic. The daylight hours were getting a touch longer and nature's colour seemed to be appearing once more, as if an age-old artist had returned from retirement to begin to paint the world again. And there was nothing like a spring in the Welsh Valleys. I was taking Jess back to my hometown to stay with my parents and to catch up with some old faces.

In less than a month's time I would be undertaking the role of usher and Master of Ceremonies at the wedding of an old school friend. A few beverages had been arranged in Cardiff as a final catch-up before the big day. Alcohol and an obsession with the Devil's Wheel were about to collide.

The familiar journey across the Severn Bridge from England to Wales began a seemingly pleasant weekend with my soulmate. After an hour of travelling, the green hills came into view and we had arrived at my childhood home. I shared the story of my recent good fortune with my parents, who congratulated me. It was not an easy time for young people in their mid-twenties to acquire their own property, and they knew all too well that this would be a great help to the cause. If only I had pondered that notion with greater attention.

Saturday arrived and we ventured into the capital by train via the Valleys Line. Cardiff was embracing a cosmopolitan blend of urbanity and cuisine as well as promoting the distinctly Welsh culture and language. We met in the bar area of a restaurant, and I was pleased to see some old faces from my childhood. Within seconds, it was as if we had never been apart. Their less-familiar partners seemed pleasant enough, and we moved to our table to order our dinner.

After several minutes of reading the elaborate, colourful menu with many wonderful food options, the waitress came across to take our order. When it was my turn...

"I'll have a boiled egg, please." To which the waitress stared blankly before the beginnings of a bewildered frown emerged across her forehead.

Some of the laughter from my faithful crowd of old friends alerted her that it was in fact a joke, despite my deadpan, stone-faced delivery. I apologised profusely for the terrible joke and proceeded to make a far more sensible order of the hottest curry available on the menu. Little did I know that it would turn out to be mild in comparison to the night of gambling to follow.

After the meal and several drinking establishments later, we all ended up at a live music venue. I began talking to a friend who was going to be the best man at the wedding in a few weeks' time. He was also a man who dabbled in the betting world – we had played many card games and accompanied each other on several casino trips in the past. We spoke intensely about my recent betting techniques, and I suddenly became eager to demonstrate.

A dreadful consequence of the modern world's "always connected" philosophy is that access is constant, and as a result, it becomes so much more difficult to establish boundaries, particularly when involving alcoholic impairment.

I pulled out my phone – a portable device for constant access to the Devil's Wheel – and signed in to the betting account. In another moment of madness, I cancelled my recent withdrawal request. The withdrawal request which included the miraculous £3,000 win. I was on very shaky ground.

I placed £100 on the first and second sets of twelve.

My good friend was bemused at my liberated, fearless disregard for the sheer scale of this bet. £200 on a single bet. Just a short time ago, it would have been inconceivable. What is most troubling about this attitude is that it was still a significant amount of money for me. But it didn't feel that way at all.

It was clear that Lady Luck was still in my corner. It would be a while before it dawned on me that my wins had been pure coincidence – something that human beings find very difficult to understand and accept.

The silver ball planted itself on a number in the middle twelve and a total of £300 made its way back into my account. My friend appeared to be amused, but Jess was not. It was the first time I had noticed her discontent with my gambling. She was usually very easy-going by nature and so that alone should have been enough of a warning. My alcohol-fuelled enthusiasm had other ideas.

Others began to notice and questioned why I was dancing around a small screen rather than being present in the moment. I continued the conversation with my old friend and bought several rounds of liquor. As the hazy mist of alcohol descended over me once more, I made my most flamboyant gambling move yet. After several more wins, I was ready to push the limits. I pressed the 500 chip symbol and proceeded to press the red section… twice. A single bet of £1,000 on red.

This decision was a milestone. Not a positive one, but a checkpoint whereby my perspective had been permanently damaged. You may consider this a strange use of language considering how much money I was winning. In fact, I would have considered it strange too. But I had lost all concept of the value of money when it came to a gambling environment.

My old friend peered over my shoulder in disbelief as we watched the ball dance around the bowl once more, and it finally landed abruptly inside the lips of the number 3 – red! My friend let out a surprised, shocked laugh and I raised the phone up in the air in hysterics whilst letting out a cheer and raising up my other hand in a victory fist.

One thousand pounds in a single spin. A matter of seconds. I was totally unaware of my surroundings. After ordering another round of drinks, I was at it again without a second's thought. It was clear that I was now under a very dark spell. Well, I remember thinking to myself, "It's now a free bet. I can go again with this one thousand pounds." I cannot stress enough how easy it is to fall into this trap when betting with what is essentially numbers on a screen. There is a total disassociation with the reality of the action.

"Phil, I think Jess would like a bit of company now…" explained the young wife-to-be, the partner of one of my childhood friends. People began to notice, and as I glanced across, I could see that my own partner in crime was hardly impressed. I did give some recognition and explained my phone battery was at six percent so I would soon be back in the room. But not before another bet.

I was awash with the feelings of freedom after far too many drinks and far too many bets. It was an awful cocktail, but in my drunken and victorious haze, I was back and on top of my game. The feeling of invincibility had somehow broken into the fabric of my own personality. The live band played some classic cover songs, but it was completely passing me by as I became more and more consumed by the gambling.

There was a brief interlude to the madness as I ordered copious amounts of alcoholic drinks for my friends – I was feeling incredibly generous given the current circumstances. I started to talk more openly about my recent activity, and I distinctly remember explaining the ridiculous £1,000 bet to another friend.

"It's a great win… but… if you'd lost, it would be the most sickening feeling." A voice of reason, and one that I should well have listened to. But I was too blinded by a false sense of security in a pseudo-blanket of profit.

The stakes were raised once more. I was going to go out with a bang before my phone battery finally died. I placed £1,000 on the second column set and a further £1,000 on the third. It was a truly significant sum of money, and money that I could have invested in causes that I really believed in. None of that reality entered my thoughts, and I proceeded to place the bet to the value of £2,000. The bet could be lost within a matter of seconds – the time from the click of the "spin" button to the landing of the silver ball within the lips of a number.

The ball landed in the third column and a further £1,000 of profit sailed into my account total. Despite this phenomenal high, it was possibly one of the worst things that could have happened – as it so often is during the experience of an addiction.

Addiction can be a difficult word, and concept, to come to terms with, and one that would take me a while to accept. I was a fairly disciplined and headstrong individual and I'd never really pushed the boundaries of excess too much up to this point. But the addiction was in the shadows.

In the heat of the moment, I was standing tall. Invincible. My winnings now surpassed £5,000. And my phone battery died. Somewhat of an anti-climax, or perhaps the best thing that could have happened to save me from myself. I was feeling quite the opposite to any notion of needing to be saved.

There was still some of the night left and the live music was still in full flow. This highlights just how quickly it can happen – winning it all or losing everything. The phenomenal win had played out within the space of minutes, stretched to an hour with the inclusion of brief interludes of conversation and ordering of drinks. Any concerns amongst friends had soon faded as I returned to the room to rejoin the gathering. I distinctly remember receiving some vital advice from my old friend, the fellow gambler who had been observing my activity that night.

"Phil, you've done well, but make sure you put on your deposit limit when you go back on…"

The deposit limit tool is available on all registered gambling sites and is a very important lifeline. It is a fail-safe that can be used to force yourself to think again. You can set a deposit limit by the day, week, or month. So if, for example, you set a monthly deposit limit of

£50, when you have reached this amount you will not be able to deposit any more funds until this resets the following month. The real fail-safe element of this is that although you can remove your own deposit limit at any given time, it takes twenty-four hours before it activates. After this twenty-four-hour period passes, you are able to confirm or reject the removal of the limit. What is absolutely key about this is that those twenty-four hours can be a significant period of reflection. Even a period of sobriety. My gambling episodes were often happening whilst under the influence of alcohol. Had I made use of the deposit limit, I would have been able to reassess my decisions with a sober mind. I cannot urge anyone to use this tool enough, even the disciplined gambler who likes an occasional flutter. Because that's exactly what I was before this journey.

It had been quite a remarkable evening. A chance for old faces to meet new faces, and a chance to reunite before an old friend embarked on a new chapter in his life. Oh, and, of course, the moment I placed the biggest single bet I could ever have dreamed of and won a sum of money that was beginning to enter the realms of life-changing.

I accompanied Jess back to the Cardiff Central train station so that we could take the Valleys Line back to my parents' home. The two-carriage train arrived and it made its way out of the city and up into the hills. What a beautiful end it might have been to both the evening as well as my gambling journey. But the highs and lows of the Devil's Wheel had only just begun.

8. THE VERY BIG WIN

"You head upstairs, and I'll bring some water up shortly," I whispered to Jess, not wanting to wake anyone up upon our return from Cardiff.

As she headed off, instead of heading to the kitchen for the water, I went straight for the computer in the study. Despite a dead phone battery, I was determined that the night's gambling was not done. This proved the seriousness of my situation – I had just won over £5,000 in a matter of hours, a very serious sum of money for a man of my age as well as my social and economic background. Even so, I didn't think it was done. In a way, I was right.

In mere minutes, I was back online and logged into the gambling website. The numbers on the screen showed my account total. I opened up the Devil's Wheel and started from exactly where I'd left off earlier in the evening. It was past 11 p.m., and although I was beginning to sober up it wasn't enough to restore my inner voice of reason.

Still possessed, I repeated the same bet from earlier that evening. I placed £1,000 on the second column set and £1,000 on the third. Yet another £2,000 stake in a single bet. The maximum stake on any individual column or section of twelve was £1,000, and there was a maximum of £2,000 on even-money bets such as red, black, odd, or even.

Things were starting to spiral badly out of control. The miraculous run of luck continued, as the ball landed in the third column AGAIN. I clenched my fist and mouthed a "yes" under my breath in satisfaction. Another £1,000 profit won in a matter of seconds. The significance of this did not cross my mind, not for a single second. On with the game...

My betting strategy to date had included changing the bet regularly in an attempt to keep up with the completely unpredictable nature of roulette. Something I had known from the start is that the previous numbers shown on the roulette wheel are purely there as entertainment. Each spin of the wheel is a brand new, independent game. The previous numbers have absolutely no bearing on anything – there is no pattern, only coincidence.

Perhaps it was some of the alcohol still in my system, but in a dazed frenzy I clicked "repeat" in order to run the same bet once more. It lost. £2,000 swallowed in a single bet. *Two... thousand... pounds.* Surely time for a line in the sand? Call it the end of a good run and walk away a winner. Not yet.

I was completely numb to the incredibly damaging loss that had just taken place – a key sign that the addiction had really taken a hold and would not relent. I carried on regardless, and instead of falling victim to a lack of patience, I was completely calm and quietly transfixed. I changed the bet to the first and second set of columns, again staking £1,000 on each column. The number 4 flashed up on the screen, putting me straight back into my winning ways.

I heard a trail of footsteps making their way down the stairs so I quickly minimised the screen and rushed out of the study into the lounge.

"What are you doing down here? Are you coming to bed now?" enquired Jess.

"Wait there," I whispered back as I made my way out to the kitchen. I returned with a pint glass of water and handed it to Jess, who had stayed at the bottom of the stairs. "I'll be up to bed in a minute. I just want to transfer the money I won into my bank account."

"Ok, don't be too long." And with that, Jess headed back up the stairs. She was still a little groggy from the night's drinking session to be any more concerned, especially as I was yet to reveal the extent of my activity so far.

I returned to the screen and the gentle movement of the resting wheel. What was to follow was something I can't imagine I would ever be able to repeat. I placed a further £1,000 on the second set of twelve and £1,000 on the third set. Another win.

I changed the patterns for the next three bets, winning each time to mark my most incredible run of victories so far and a total profit of over £8,000. The startling sum of money did not sink in; it was just a set of numbers on a screen. It left me daring to push the limits of the game once more.

My next bet was £1,000 on the middle column, £1,000 on the third column, and another £1,000 on red. Three thousand pounds on a single bet by a man completely possessed and out of control. My eyes spun as fast as the wheel as they tracked the ball like a heat-seeking missile... BANG! The number 18 – red and appearing in the third column. I had just won £2,000 of profit in a single bet, in a couple of seconds. The feeling of euphoria and invincibility finally broke my calm hypnosis, and my hands began to shake.

Before I had time to process my actions and emotions, I placed a further £1,000 onto black. I was now using the £1,000 chip as if it was pocket change, which is remarkable given that I had never accumulated any kind of wealth in my life, other than a small amount of savings I had been building up for the future. I really believe that it was a combination of the detachment from reality that comes with online gambling and my own lack of interest in material wealth that drove me to keep betting.

The appearance of the red number 36 was my first loss in the last seven or eight bets, and the total in my account shrunk by £1,000. It felt completely insignificant – I was up by thousands, and I would win it back.

I put no more faith in betting on anything that presented less than a 50% chance of success and reverted to the column and section betting. The risk with this tactic was that my stake was £2,000, and any losing streak would threaten total wipe-out.

A hat-trick of wins followed, and I had now accumulated a profit of over £12,000. Before that life-changing figure could sink in, a message popped up on the screen:

Would you like to change your table stakes to Maximum: £4,000?

Yes / No

I clicked "No" – £4,000 was an obscene amount. I was relieved that despite my apparent loss of all reason I was able to find some kind of sense that had been otherwise clouded by the gambling storm.

The option to increase the maximum is not a function available to all customers. My excessive betting and spending had prompted the demons in the system to come out with further temptations to eat into my very soul. It is clear that gambling companies are actively encouraging addiction and the front they so cleverly put on with their so-called firewalls is laughable – the gambler is left to their own devices with regard to deposit limits and other self-regulating methods. Gambling companies are nothing more than ultra-capitalist, legal drug dealers, feeding on the vulnerabilities of the general populace.

I lost the next bet and I told myself that, should I lose the one after, my work would be done and I would stop at a grand total of £10,000. It was now well past midnight and sobriety was inching ever closer as I downed another glass of water. I didn't lose the next bet, nor the next. The streak of good fortune had a precarious shelf life that I was pushing ever closer to with each bet. I could sense the end was coming as several losses began to accompany the wins.

The good kind of luck still seemed to just about be fighting my corner, and its final round proved to be the most explosive. A daring bet of £1,000 on the first column, £1,000 on the second, along with £1,000 on the first section of twelve and a final £1,000 on the third section saw me risking a total of £4,000. All on the spin of a wheel.

I began to feel more and more dizzy with the spinning of the wheel, and I could feel the heaviness in my eyes willing me to finish it. The metal ball fell into place on one of the numbers in the first section of twelve, in the second column. It satisfied the necessary aspects of my bet for the highest possible return – £4,000 of profit. It brought my total win to the sum of £20,000. A monumental moment. A life-changing sum of money that would undoubtedly be celebrated in style.

I gave a wry smirk as I saw the numbers on the screen, but that was all I could seem to manage. It was as if I knew that there was something disingenuous about the otherwise spectacular win. Take away the remarkable run of good luck, and the behaviour itself was very self-destructive and damaging in terms of loss of control, addiction, and the detached relationship with the numbers on the screen.

But all that aside, that night I was a winner. A very big winner.

9. "TO GOOD HEALTH AND PROSPERITY…"

The next few days were electric. I felt one hundred feet tall – unconquerable. I had just taken on the house and beaten them, despite the odds being stacked. After sharing the news with my close family, I returned to Bristol with the world at my feet.

I revealed the good news to one of my housemates, who was in total disbelief at the sum of the win.

"That's unbelievable – congratulations!" he announced sincerely.

"I'm definitely stopping it there though. I've withdrawn the money now," I replied with complete conviction.

"I wish I'd done the same when I had a big win from a football bet."

"When was that?"

"Years ago," he explained. "It wasn't anywhere near yours, but it was a few thousand. I kept betting with it and only walked away when I'd spent all the winnings."

"That must have been absolutely gutting!"

"Yeah, it was! Just don't do it, mate. Just don't."

"Definitely not," I confirmed. It would be the investment of a lifetime, and the future had never looked so bright.

After withdrawing the £20,000 of profit from my betting account, I was left with an odd £37 remaining. I placed it on a football bet, really just to have some fun with the last funds before walking away. I used a similar all-or-nothing approach and placed the money on Manchester United to win. The odds were dreadful, roughly equivalent to 0.4–1, which gave me almost £15 of profit. I withdrew this last bit of money, but it planted a seed about a different kind of betting. A seed that would later begin its growth.

Jess's birthday was fast approaching, and prior to my big win I had arranged a weekend in Pembrokeshire on the south-west coast of Wales. I was sure that the recent win was going to bring with it many travels to far-off lands, but until then I was going to make sure that I pulled out all the stops to celebrate the beginning of a new era.

We walked along the beautiful coast, and the April sun shone down on the luckiest man in the world. We dined in a nice little local restaurant with all expenses covered. We drank to the sound of hearty, live folk music in a nearby pub and walked our way through the historic town walls to sit amongst the ruins of the castle at moonrise.

On the final day of our weekend, I arranged a boat trip to the nearby Caldey Island, whose only residents are a community of Cistercian monks. I had last visited as a small child, and now I was returning at such a landmark moment, it seemed a fitting place to discuss the future. After buying a cold drink from the island cafe and finding a nice spot of shade outside, we began to talk of the big bright highway ahead, and the head start that this sudden influx of fortune could bring us.

I had always firmly believed that, as once told to me by my wise old grandmother, "health is wealth." But with seemingly insurmountable property prices and the ever-increasing cost of living, a head start in that department offered a huge sense of relief and freedom.

We went on to talk about all of the places in the world we would like to visit, and the hours rolled by to the sound of the birds that brought the island to life. With that, we headed for the monastery for a service – for the spiritual experience rather than religious purposes.

The voices of the monks soothed the soul, and we proceeded to a vantage point in an old tower that looked back towards the mainland. There in the tower lay an open book with messages of goodwill. I took the pen and left my mark…

To good health and prosperity… all the best.

It was my well wishes for the islanders, but it was also exactly what I saw ahead for us. All of the things I'd considered to be holding me back had become irrelevant. The everyday frustrations at my place of work, the attitudes of others, and the stresses of shared accommodation were just old cobwebs that had become dust in the wind.

Another week passed and I had begun to search for new properties, both in Bristol and just the other side of the border in Monmouthshire. I considered all of the people who had always supported me throughout my life; I advised my parents that I could return to them the £1,000 sum that I would receive from the sale of my late grandmother's house. I also transferred a £500 sum to my sister's account as a gesture.

I look back on that now and realise these gestures were nothing compared to the money I had just amassed. It seems, in a way, greedy. Yes, I had no obligation to give anything, but it had always been in my nature to be charitable. The problem was that I had not only lost all concept of the value of money, but I had never found myself with any kind of wealth in my life thus far, so I did not really understand what I was to do with it.

The end of April could not have been sweeter, and I was contacted by some friends to catch up over a few beers. Jess had similar plans with her own friends, so I finished work and headed back to my family home once again. I was looking forward to sharing my good news and generously buying rounds of drinks that were comparatively much cheaper in the valleys of south Wales. I was blissfully unaware that the devil would visit me again very soon.

10. A DEADLY COCKTAIL

I was standing at that old bus stop. The one I had always stood at, day after day to wait for the beaten-up old school bus, or for trips to the centre of Cardiff, or days out to the coast. Or, like tonight, many Friday evenings at an old social club in a village a few miles away. Here I was again, despite the twists and turns of life so far. Here I was again.

The old stomping ground was typical of a Welsh Valley social club. From the outside it looked like a bomb-damaged hostel, and the inside was something of a time warp – stuck in a bygone era from some time in the middle of the 20th century. There was a mixture of clientele at the club: the old stalwarts that had sat in the same seats for forty years or more, the young guns who should probably still be on soft drinks, but there were also occasional groups of unsavoury characters that floated in from other nearby taverns to use and deal drugs. Believe it or not, this particular club was slightly more inviting than some of the cesspits in the area.

All of these colourful characters aside, I had often met there with friends on Friday evenings to drown out the troubles of the week with a few pints of ale. It had been a constant (though sometimes begrudgingly) place of belonging. Whilst my old world was changing and I was starting new chapters, I had this one place of familiarity.

I made my way inside and headed towards the bar. A young man who I vaguely recognised appeared to remember me very fondly. I had no doubt it was mistaken identity, but I nonetheless played along whilst awaiting my beer, despite his persistently loud and incoherent ramblings. He looked as though he may have been indulging in more than just a few pints. Thankfully, I spotted an old friend walking through the entrance to the bar and breathed a sigh of relief. I could finally unwind with more suitable company. We shook hands and I called for an extra pint before heading to the tables beyond the bar.

Although I was on top of the world with my recent good fortune, I felt a bit disillusioned by the circumstances that had befallen some of the old faces. I had been lucky enough to have a stable family so I could broaden my own horizons, but some of the people here, even the ones I was associating with, were spiralling into a life of regular drug use and unemployment, really bordering on a cycle of despair. It began to get to me but, as I would come to realise, temptation comes in many guises; just as they were slipping into oblivion, I was becoming engulfed by a gambling addiction.

A few people, some of whom were my friends, were outside in the smoking areas, a few at the bar, and some at the toilet – either doing what you are supposed to do at the toilet, or indulging in some Colombian marching powder (probably about ninety percent washing up powder by the time the local dealers had dished it all out). I turned my conversation to one of the few people left at my table, a well-known drug user who had just made a call for his evening's supply.

I had spoken with the chap a few times before, and if you got past the haze of drugs and alcohol, there was much more to him. I've always thought it important to try to find these things in people. Whilst there might be an element of personal accountability in their problems, you don't really know the choices on the table, the circumstances, the upbringing and families, and the disadvantages in these forgotten valleys, without really living it yourself. It's often too much to overcome, particularly in socially and economically deprived areas such as this.

Unfortunately, the young man at the bar at the beginning of the night had found his way to our table and continued to shout about his troubles, although he was largely incoherent. Some of the older stalwarts became agitated, and I can understand why. My friends and I did not really want to be associated with him, but we tried, and failed, to calm him down. I started to question why I bothered with the place anymore. Perhaps I had to find a way to move on.

My feeling of displacement was exacerbated by my decision to leave my hometown to find greater opportunities. On the one hand, I felt a deep attachment to home, but this was simultaneously contradicted with feelings of despair, resentment, and disillusionment. It also meant that when I ventured forth to new worlds, I was faced with difficulty in connecting with those from more comfortable circles. I've never truly found a solution, but I will continue to contemplate this dilemma.

A few more friends had joined us, but the evening still felt lifeless. A few old jingles rang out from the jukebox, and I shared the news of my recent win to a few people who briefly congratulated me but seemed otherwise disinterested. I suppose it didn't really matter to them. Nothing seemed to matter to them. I began to feel slightly philosophical again, in a melancholic kind of way. Life here had taken away a real sense of purpose from people.

I decided to try to calm the agitated young man as a voice of reason, but he began to threaten me. I could see he was not really in a fit state to cause any real trouble, to me or any of the others, but he was not worth any more effort. He was advised by the steward that he would be asked to leave if he continued with his disruptive behaviour.

I turned my back on the hopeless man, but was faced only with more hopeless conversation as the young men to my other side were discussing some of their drug-related escapades.

"Two double brandies please, John," I asked the barman. I drank them like a parched vagabond and ordered two more, as well as a pint of cold beer to take back to my seat. That's when the cocktail began to stir, and subsequently shake, inside my head.

I took my phone out of my pocket and looked at it pensively. Searching for some sort of solace in the screen that was staring back at me. I made no effort to speak anymore, and it was reciprocated as those loosely in my company continued to busy themselves in their conversations.

I will never truly know why I then made the decision to log in to my gambling account, but with the benefit of hindsight, it was a momentary loss of self in negative surroundings, the feeling of accepted despair amongst people, and the obvious addition of too much drink. But it was more than just that. My gambling pursuits up to this point had been astoundingly successful. Life changing. And they made me feel like a man on top of his game – on top of the world. But that was a temporary illusion. It had opened up some gaping vulnerabilities. Dependencies. It was the proof that in times of low mood or depression, gambling could be a saviour. A way out. To be a winner.

11. DRINKING WITH THE DEVIL

There it was. That old silver ball floating on the screen. And I knew the game. I knew my strategy. I knew how to win. I pressed "Deposit Now" and racked the number up to £1,000 to place straight onto red. The ball seemed to spin twice as fast as usual and stopped dead at number 33. Black. A thousand pounds sucked into the void. A horrible, churning dread filled my stomach, but it quickly vanished when I realised I was not really going to lose – I was too far ahead!

Suddenly, I was no longer in the room. I was at the wheel. Driving. In control. The next time it was £2,000 on red. A consecutive number occurred, where the result repeated, and the silver ball fell into 33 black again. A consecutive result can work in your favour if you are betting on individual numbers rather than sections – for me, it was not good news as my strategy up to that point had mostly been to keep things varied. I was furious. £3,000 – a staggering amount of money – had just vanished from my bank account in a matter of minutes. I would not stand for that.

I put my phone away temporarily and looked around. I noticed that some people had left the club, and I shook the hand of someone who was just about to leave. I ordered yet another beer at the bar, and whilst patiently awaiting the pouring of my pint from the pump, I glanced over to the table I had been sitting at. It was empty. The few stalwarts of the group, who would hang around for a conversational encore after the last orders, had gathered at a more brightly lit table.

I sat down opposite the young man I had been discussing philosophical nonsense with earlier in the evening – he was one of the few people left that I really recognised. He continued to slur a few stories about the drug-induced escapades of his past, at which point I began to discuss my gambling pursuits.

After very little reciprocated interest, I pulled out my phone once again and returned to the roulette wheel. The alcohol was whirling through my bloodstream, and my thoughts and reasoning were disappearing with each sip of beer. It was half past eleven, and the call for last orders passed me by as I sat in my trance.

Somewhere within the drunken chambers of my mind, the demon awakened with all its might. I would not accept that £3,000 loss. I could not – I was untouchable. I had won far too much to have anything to risk. How wrong that naive viewpoint was. And I was mature enough and sensible enough to know that – but I was not in a sober state of mind and that made a significant difference.

I deposited the entirety of my profits into the

gambling site, which was now £17,000 after the £3,000 loss from earlier in the evening. I won the following bet but lost the next. Thankfully, my good fortune then showed its beautiful face again, and after winning four consecutive bets I was back on track!

But I didn't feel much joy in it by that time. Somehow, the problem I had developed was becoming a routine instead of a thrill. Without the perceived risk, there was no exhilaration. And that was probably the worst time for the unsolicited pop-up to arrive again. As if it was questioning my commitment to the addiction, it dared me once more…

Would you like to change your table stakes to Maximum: £4,000?

Yes / No

I took a glance around the bar area, and the bar staff were clearing away the tables at the far end. It was almost midnight, and the final night bus would be passing the place in around half an hour. I was barely conscious of that as I clicked "Yes" to confirm the staggering increase in stakes.

It seems I was consumed. Metamorphosing into an entity that my sober self would not even recognise. For now, though, I was still a winner. A huge winner. I placed a sum of £4,000 on the first set of twelve, and £4,000 on the second. £8,000 on a single spin was obscene. Preposterous! The trouble was that I had never really begun to spend the money. I had no concept of it, and the nature of online gambling – the removal of the physical transaction, of handing something over in exchange for something else – removed a psychological barrier of restraint.

I had always known that the physical existence of currency was simply a shared illusion. Just a printed paper carrying a promise to pay the bearer; it didn't really exist. It was just a manifestation of value. Without it, I had granted myself the freedom to take risks. Risks that, if they didn't pay off, would be devastating to myself and those around me.

I pressed "Bet" and time stopped in a freeze frame. The only thing to break me from my glassy stare was the tapping and tapping of my right leg in fearful anticipation. The ball landed in number 24. I'd just about made it. A £4,000 win in a single spin. It was a life-changing amount of money, let alone in addition to the profit I had already amassed. Startlingly, I still couldn't stop.

The castle of my old self was shattered into crumbling ruins and the devil had taken the reins to wage all-out war. I finished my final beer and placed £4,000 on the middle column and £4,000 on the third. The ball landed in number 5, gifting me another £4,000.

I barely batted an eyelid and clicked the "Repeat Bet" option. The ball whizzed around in its usual frenzy and the consecutive results phenomenon worked in my favour as the ball landed once again in the number 5. A further £4,000 profit resulted in a total profit of £38,000.

I felt a wave of emotion and slammed my fist onto

the table, startling my only companion left that evening – the recreational drug user I had spoken to throughout the night. I showed him the screen on my phone and pointed to the figure. He looked at it through his drunken glaze and chuckled loudly whilst tilting his head back. I'm not sure he'd really taken it in.

My relentless quest for the next milestone added to my refusal to draw a line in the sand. The untamed beast in the basement of my belly wanted to take its final bite – I had won £38,000, so I could win £40,000 and round that off as another extraordinary chapter in my seemingly endless victory against the house.

It was five minutes until midnight. Only a small corner of the social club had anyone left in it. A few old stragglers in quiet conversation, and two heavily drunk and drugged-up young men to my right. It would have to be my last bet, or else it would be a very long walk home at the dead of night. I reduced my bet to £2,000. (No, I never thought I would ever use the word "reduced" when describing the sum of £2,000 either.) I placed it onto black and kept my fingers crossed. My drunken memory will not allow me to recall the number on this occasion, but I know it was a red number because I lost the bet.

"Argh," I mumbled under my breath.

I took a moment to look away from the screen. Despite always fighting against the sheep-like mentality of the modern human being, I couldn't help thinking that anyone observing me would see me as a typical twenty-something glued to my phone. I moved my heavy head and stared longingly at my empty pint glass.

The £36,000 in the corner of my screen soon snapped me out of my half-slumber and back to the reality of my great victory. I was unstoppable, and I would reach that unthinkable milestone of £40,000.

I went straight back into the high stakes. £4,000 on the first column, £4,000 on the second. I lost. £8,000 in a couple of seconds. I clicked "Repeat Bet". I lost again. That was £16,000, vanished in the few minutes that separated Friday night from Saturday morning. There was no promise of a new dawn for me. That was the biggest gambling mistake I had ever made. When there is a subtle sign that the tables have turned, a bet made out of impatience and rushing to "put things right" is a sure way to fall headfirst into demise.

I had a torrid addiction that I had not even acknowledged, and that is why I couldn't stop. But before I could continue with the terrible affliction, I remembered the final bus was close and so I waved goodbye to the inhabitants of the social club – it was always a while between visits by this point, although I'm not sure the few left inside even realised I was leaving.

I waited at the bus stop across the road, just a few buildings away, outside a nightclub that had closed down a few years previously. The last night bus was usually around ten past midnight, and as I waited, I placed two further bets – winning the first, losing the second, no ground was made. In my alcohol-clouded mess, I had completely forgotten that despite losing a truly shocking £16,000 out of that evening's winnings, I still had the £20,000 of profit.

The bus was fashionably late, and although I'm not

sure its timely arrival would have saved me from myself, it might have been a helpful distraction. I continued the complete train wreck of self-destruction. I seemed to be suffering a serious state of detachment from my own personality, which again creates a comparison to a very dangerous misuse of toxic substances. Of course, alcohol was playing its part, but there was a deeper issue that I had failed to realise.

I proceeded to place a further two bets in the same fashion. £4,000 on the first twelve, £4,000 on the second twelve. How on earth could I possibly go through with this staggering act of stupidity? How on earth had it gone this far? I was betting a truly life-changing sum of money, £8,000, on a single spin. The bet lost. And all control was lost. I clicked "Repeat" and lost again. £16,000 lost in five minutes. Five minutes standing at a bus stop, with no physical transaction or money changing hands. I had just lost £32,000 of my good fortune in less than half an hour.

The bus emerged from the bend in the road with its glowing orange sign displaying "*Tonypandy*". I scrambled around my pocket for my return ticket. Despite the bus journey being one of my most familiar routes, that night I could not have been more lost. I slouched into a seat midway down the carriage. Amidst the chattering of drunken locals heading home, I stared out of the large window and into the night. Empty.

***

I was back at my family home in a blur, but my sobering

thoughts had not managed to break the spell I was under. Every ounce of myself was drowning in this addiction. I find it hard to believe that this was actually me, these were my actions. It seems so far removed from who I am and who I thought I was.

Rage soon followed the feelings of despair, and a volcano of anger erupted from within and completely engulfed me. I headed straight for the study and switched on the computer. I deposited the remainder of my winnings, which was £4,000 by this point. Though I'd only had my winnings for a short time, I seemed convinced that it was now pocket change. In reality, it was still a sum of money that would have had a massive impact upon my life, and I knew many people from my walk of life who needed it even more. This is something that would plague my thoughts in the time to follow.

I was forced to reduce my bets to £2,000 per section, but in terms of strategy, I continued in the same vein. The horrible reversal of fortunes also continued, and in seconds I had lost all of the profit. I stared intensely at the screen, and I could hear voices in my head as clearly as if they were in the room with me…

"Just don't do it, mate. Just don't."

"Phil, you've done well, but make sure you put on your deposit limit."

Instead of heeding the advice of these voices of reason, I became disgusted with myself. The disgust manifested itself in anger that was undoubtedly exacerbated by the alcohol.

I opened up a new window on the computer and logged in to my online banking to see the live balance figure had been reduced to nothing. Below that was the figure representing my life savings. It is perhaps a humble figure to some of the world's highfliers, but to a man from my background, it was a significant sum. As I have so often stated, I didn't care much for the material things in life, nor for money itself, but I was building up enough to further my travels with Jess and to secure some place that we might be able to call our own.

The £9,000 that I had secured mostly from my own earnings also included an inheritance from the sale of my grandmothers' houses – £1,000 from each, for which I was eternally grateful. It was to be a foundation to plan for my future. But tonight, I was not in control of it. Instead, it would be in the hands of whoever had possessed my soul. Although, the cold, hard truth is that that was me. I was doing this. I deposited the entirety of the savings into the betting account. I just could not stop. I was vengeful, desperate, and completely deluded in a chaotic storm of alcohol and gambling. I didn't even have the sense to get myself a drink of water.

I continued to bet with £2,000 on each section, and two victories lit a stirring hope. This is where I must highlight the sickening danger of gambling – a temporary run of wins amidst a heavy loss is absolutely fundamental to the formula of the house. Ultimately, you will lose – the laws of probability cannot be broken. The longer you play, the more likely it is you will lose. And I was playing, and playing, and with each and every painstaking spin of the wheel, I was tipping myself closer and closer to the cliff edge.

Those last two victories were very much the

beginning of the end. Three consecutive losses followed from bets using that same old formula. £1,000 remained – and that is when I did the unthinkable. I deposited a further £2,000 I didn't actually have. My arranged overdraft – a contingency I had rarely ever used. I can remember dipping into it to help fund my initial move to Bristol, but that was resolved after a few months of wages. I willingly placed the entirety of the £3,000 onto red. That's when everything turned black.

12. HERO TO ZERO

In a matter of hours, I had spent the £38,000 of my incredible fortune, along with £9,000 of my life savings and inheritance – some of which I had promised to return to my parents following my big win – and a further £2,000 of my arranged overdraft. The total of £49,000 was absolutely ludicrous. A sum that I would never have imagined ever being in possession of, let alone in my mid-twenties. And I had just spun it all away in one evening.

All I could do was bury my head in my hands. Sobriety seemed to have been accelerated by the stark reality of the situation I found myself in. It was as if the devil's work was done and only now would it relinquish its hold over me. I ran to the bathroom and came close to being sick – perhaps that was the devil escaping. But, more frighteningly, there was no devil. There was only me.

I began to pace the room in despair. To stop myself imploding and making any further mistakes, I called

Jess.

"It's gone. I've lost everything." I remember fumbling over my words.

Jess was out with friends, on her journey home in the twilight hours. At first it was met with an awkward laugh. No doubt she was convinced that it was just another one of my silly jokes. I persisted and shared my distress, and, remarkably, she remained a pillar of strength and reason despite the obviously upsetting burden of bad news. I stared blankly at the ceiling whilst lying on my bed for the remainder of the twilight hours before Saturday morning rose. I wondered if I would ever rise again.

***

I rarely came home to visit just for a few pints of ale in an old social club. I was also back for the wedding of the couple we had met up with in Cardiff just a few months ago. I was going to be an usher and Master of Ceremonies and would spend the evening before Sunday's wedding with the groom, best man, and the second usher – all of whom were old friends. Jess would be joining me at the church in Port Talbot before the evening's celebration followed in Cowbridge.

Painfully, the plan was to play a few games of poker the evening before the big day. Usually it would have been perfect – but I did not know how I would bring myself to play. The best man was the one to have advised me of the deposit limit just weeks before my catastrophic capitulation occurred. How could I face my friends after sharing the news of my great win with them just over a week ago?

I spoke with Jess again in the morning. She was going to spend the evening before the wedding with my parents. Thankfully, she agreed that it was not the time to share the bad news with my family… yet. I had to piece myself together first.

The groom-to-be dealt out the cards, and it was just like old times. I had managed to freshen up from the previous evening and I had no choice but to forget absolutely everything for the next two days. I didn't matter. I was there to do a duty for an old friend.

A few hands rolled by in quite a friendly fashion, and then I was dealt a nine and ten of clubs, the hand that had catapulted me into the world of serious gambling three years earlier in Amsterdam. I looked down at the table but I wasn't seeing anything there, I was seeing and feeling the warmth and thrill of the win in the Dutch capital. A world away from where and who I was now.

I folded because I couldn't bear to play the hand. And that set the tone for the rest of the night as I lost both games. We played for £5 total stake each game and that all just seemed so completely meaningless now.

"I guess my luck just isn't in tonight," I announced after being knocked out of the second game.

"Ah well, you can't be twenty grand up every night!" said my fellow usher.

I couldn't bring myself to tell him the truth, and instead I somehow mustered a smile before quickly changing the subject.

I drank some beer in hope of putting my desolation aside, and I was relieved to get the poker games out of the way. I could face myself after the weekend. We tuned in to a world heavyweight title boxing match, and as the main event began, I watched the boxers exchanging punches. Right now, in my own life, I was flat out on the canvas. If I could get up, there'd be plenty more hits and falls. Although at this time, I hadn't even considered the long-term psychological damage of recent events.

I was delighted when Jess arrived at the church. I knew she would help me to hold together the shattered pieces of myself, at least for the weekend. A weekend that was not about me at all. I wish I had been able to really forget. I wish I could have been generously buying rounds of drinks to celebrate a great new chapter, but in reality I could not escape my regret and self-loathing.

The pleasant ceremony passed by in a blink and we were on route to Cowbridge for an evening of food, drink, speeches, and plenty more drink. Although alcohol had played a part in my misjudgements, it provided some solace to help me put myself aside for that day and to carry out my duty. I guided the guests around, collected gifts, and introduced the speech-makers, even managing a few light-hearted jokes.

I remained reserved and on good behaviour. Though, there were moments where Jess had to pull me back into the room from being phased out in deep, pensive reflection.

It was time to show the self-restraint that I had always prided myself on in the past, and I turned down another drink in favour of heading back to our hotel room. My duty here was done and now it was time to figure out how on earth I would get back up from the canvas.

13. THE FALLOUT

I'd returned to Bristol at the end of the weekend. I was lying on my back, staring at the ceiling from my bed again. Jess had returned to her family home, and I was left to face up to the reality of my situation. I had nothing to my name. Worse than that, I had no money to pay the rent because I had used up the £2,000 of my arranged overdraft. Jess loaned me £1,000 of her hard-earned savings, for which I was incredibly grateful and vowed unequivocally to pay back from my next pay packet.

When I finally fell asleep that Sunday night, I was perturbed by twisted dreams, one of which included a terrifying vision of my long-gone relatives glaring at me with disappointment from beyond the veil. The silver ball of the roulette wheel hurtled towards me, and I was running, and running… ARGHHHHHHH!!! I jumped up in the bed, wide awake with my heart beating furiously in my chest.

"Sounds like you had a rough night – heard you

groaning in your sleep," said my housemate later that morning.

Once again, I couldn't find the words to tell him the truth about my current situation. Recurring nightmares and sleepless nights would become a new routine.

The bank holiday weekend was coming to an end, and Jess came over later in the day as she often did during my time at the shared accommodation. She was there with me as I announced the news to my parents, and we both found it to be very upsetting. I really had lost myself in a destructive addiction, and my parents bailed me out with a loan of £2,000 – a significant chunk of their savings. I was now £3,000 in debt and I had thrown away everything I had been building up for, and more. I had thrown away the opportunity to put down a deposit on a property to begin the rest of our lives in. I could have finally moved out of rented, shared accommodation. I had been gifted a position that very few young men who had grown up in socially and economically disadvantaged areas would ever have been lucky enough to attain. Everything I thought I stood for, I'd ignored; all of the poisons in the underbelly of capitalism that had repulsed me had now consumed me. All of my confidence, belief in my own self-discipline, and the foundations that I had worked hard to build now felt completely meaningless.

After revealing the news to my parents, I was soon sent condolences from my sister, who was very sympathetic and loaned me £500 to help get me through this sticky patch. I am certain that the determination to pay everyone back for their generous support gave me some kind of push not to fall further into the pit of depressed self-loathing.

I worked long hours in the week that followed, unable to face the reality of my own personal life. I had to turn down social plans and events with made-up excuses. The next few months would be spent just working to exist, and working to right the wrongs of one fatal evening. The heart of the matter was that it was not just the result of one evening but an extended spree of a gambling addiction that I had lost control of long before I had actually started losing. I should never have been betting with those kinds of stakes in the first place. The spiral effect of a gambling addiction can entrap you with a false perspective on the value of money, a perspective completely detached from any true reality.

More marriages were on the horizon for some of my friends, and another was arranging a huge event for their stag party. A trip to Las Vegas. I had to decline what would have been quite a chapter in my gambling journey with the lame excuse that I was unable to get the time off.

Everything began to take a negative spin. It would be years before I could even recoup my life savings. A big problem for a gambler is, much like with any other addiction, the recovery is a very long road. My catastrophic loss and self-destruction was the only point I had acknowledged that it was out of control. I still had the privilege of a loving family, food, warmth, and shelter. Who was I to feel like this was a difficult experience? But it had all lost its meaning and only added to the self-deprecation and loathing.

The fallout of the psychological damage manifested itself in the beginning of a further downfall. As soon as the weekend arrived, I returned to the wheel.

I still had not had the time to process what had really happened before. The true value of the sums of money still had not hit home. How could I sit there seriously and bet with five or ten pounds, or even a hundred? It was completely insignificant. I had been on top of the world, up there in the dizzying heights of thousand-pound stakes.

If I had begun the journey with just a small stake, I could surely do it all again with a head start. I deposited £1,000 into my account, and I was betting with a clear mind, a sober mind. I was certain I could put things right. The difference now was that I was not betting with a right mind – it had suffered the trauma of recent events, and I didn't fully realise it. After the feelings of desperation came determination. A renewed delusion that I could repeat an unrepeatable stroke of luck.

Using the same old routine of mixing up big even-money bets, £1,000 turned into £3,000 in a matter of minutes. I'm going to come back, I kept trying to convince myself. This whole situation, this loss, it just couldn't happen to me – who was that possessed young man, and who had stolen my soul?

I lost the next bet, but proceeded to win the following three. I had now recouped £5,000 in the space of twenty minutes. I could instantly pay back all of the kind people who had made their donations to me – (shockingly) this was their stake money after all.

It wasn't enough.

I took a walk to the local shop to stock up on a few essentials, and even then, I was unable to pull myself out of it. I used my phone to continue the betting. The addiction had consumed me completely. At the time, I did not realise quite how much, but I was beginning to undergo a metamorphosis. I would never be the person I was before I took the plunge into the world of serious gambling. The next handful of bets cemented me deeply in the undergrowth of the addiction. I returned from the shop in disbelief and my hands were shaking. I'd lost the entirety of the £5,000.

And what now? £3,500 in debt with no money to my name. I was becoming the very thing I had previously scorned: a foolish young man of the 21st century turning to the bank of his parents to bail him out. Worse still, my parents had never had any real wealth and now they were having to part ways with hard-earned savings.

I made the call, requesting another £2,000 bailout, not speaking a word about the events the previous evening. I simply explained that I had miscalculated my finances – an untruth on the slippery slope to nowhere. After vowing to pay back the entirety of debt in a matter of months, I realised I was reaching a breaking point, all the while keeping up a front in the general routine of everyday life.

A week of long hours passed. Appallingly, all it took was four bottles of beer for me to return to the wheel in what would prove to be a moment of huge significance. There I was again, convincing myself – with just a touch of alcohol-induced delusion – that I would right my wrongs by making the same mistakes. I had no money to my own name; the extra £2,000 bailout just covered the bank overdraft, but I placed one thousand pounds of my overdraft onto black. As I watched the silver ball spin, I realised it was mocking me, condemning me. It laughed at me as it fell into the jaws of a red number. I rose from my seat and smashed my fist into the partition wall of the bedroom in my shared accommodation, leaving a gaping black hole that I suddenly wished would swallow me up. The game was over.

14. SPECULATE TO ACCUMULATE

I felt the blood flow through my head as if it was close to boiling point. The particular hole in the wall in front of me was very different from the kind I was used to – no money was being dispensed here. I sat on my bed in defeat and watched the roulette wheel, where the ball sat lifeless, still in the jaws of a red number.

I had lost all of the money I had and more. No one else I knew had any more to give me. Surely there could have been only one solution – to stop, right then, for good. I didn't.

My hands shook as I pressed the button – what on earth was going on? What had I become? How could I face the light of day again after this? In a reluctant, distressed fit of disgust, I bet again. £1,000 on red. I took the biggest gulp of my life.

I won. It is with much regret that I tell you I dared to repeat a similar bet a further two times, on both red and black respectively, and won on both occasions. I withdrew the £4,000 and, somewhere out of the very depths of despair, the last remnants of my soul rose, and I vowed never to return to the wheel. Irreversible damage had been inflicted on my psyche, but somehow I knew at this moment I had been handed one last ticket to some kind of redemption.

This was another point in the journey that I should have walked away. In some ways, I did. It was a moment of surrender. A partial acknowledgement of the loss. The shock to my system had finally stopped me, just before the point of total self-destruct. Compared to many gamblers, many addicts, I was, in the only way I could possibly put it, lucky.

I have always believed that the greatest challenges in life start with the smallest steps. I knew that the perfect place for me to start was to fix that little hole in the wall. I felt plenty more holes in myself at the time, and no doubt there were more in those I had dragged down with me. But they would be dealt with in time. Right then, I just had to promise to myself that there would be no more business with the Devil's Wheel, and to fix up that hole in the wall.

Another summer's dream came and went, and as much as I carried myself around as if nothing had really changed, I was weary. The whole time, I was weary. I felt a big black cloud weighing down upon my shoulders every day. So tired. But, true to the promise I had made to myself, I did not return to the deathly pull of the roulette wheel. With the strength of Jess and my family, I knew that there had to be a better way out. But my spark had definitely gone; my quiet confidence had withered into yesterday. I was getting on with things, and as far as most friends and colleagues were concerned, nothing had changed.

I tried to focus on reconnecting with the things that really mattered to me: my relationships, my diet and exercise, hikes out in nature, and a minimalist approach to an otherwise material world. I secured a further promotion by working hard and preparing vigorously for the application process. It came with a pay rise, and every time I was paid by my employer, I paid back large instalments of my debt to those who had been so very kind to me.

In just six months, I had cleared my bank overdraft and paid back Jess, my sister, and my parents. Yet every single day of those six months, I woke up every morning and thought about everything that had happened. I recalled the idyllic day in Pembrokeshire, the fateful night at the social club just a week later, and I saw myself punching the wall at the point of no return. Every day it hung over me. What I could have done with the money, not just for myself but for those around me and even beyond that? I had sold out on everything I thought I had stood for.

In the end, those thoughts got the better of me. I had been so frightened by the loss of control I had experienced at the roulette wheel that I turned my attention to a slower system of betting... I began to contemplate sporting accumulators. Apart from the one I had placed shortly after my incredible win, I had only ever placed a handful of football bets in my lifetime, usually amounting to about one or two pounds each and rarely coming anywhere near a win.

How could I have possibly been contemplating gambling after everything that had happened? Well, its hold over me had been there the whole time. Not just daily thoughts and flashbacks, but reminders that came with every opportunity I had to turn down due to my unwavering commitment to paying back my debts. Despite the feeling that I had turned a corner and turned my back on the evils of roulette, I still hadn't found my way out.

It started with football matches and a strategy of betting on the favourites. I no longer had the money for the stakes I had become accustomed to, so I picked enough games to give me big odds. I placed several bets each weekend, consisting of roughly nine or ten football matches, most of which were on favourites. Sometimes I mixed it up with some close outsiders but kept them at relatively short odds. However, the nine or ten games together as an accumulator bet often resulted in odds of anywhere between 250–1 and 750–1. It seemed to satisfy my delusion – that placing a ten-pound stake on these kinds of accumulators would give me a satisfactory return of several thousands of pounds. The fallacy there was that the likelihood of all the results being correct was impossibly slim. There was also the added factor of every match having three possible outcomes: win, lose, or draw. The odds were stacked, and I knew it – and most gamblers know it – but the illusion of the ticket has an unfortunate hypnosis. The tickets gave me false hope, a constant possibility of redemption like a carrot dangling on the mirage of a long-gone sunset.

The football season was drawing to a close, but I kept buying those tickets throughout the final few weeks. I was throwing away thirty, forty pounds a week on everything I despised. Giving it to the devils of capitalism and losing the passion for all the things I believed I had stood for in the past. As long as I could keep it quiet and carry it myself, then I could announce a great victory when it happened. That was the lie that would feed my thoughts for the next few months.

The summer was fast approaching, and I had wasted several hundreds of pounds over the course of the last few months, and it was weighing down hard on me. I was still at the shared accommodation in Bristol with no sign of change any time soon. The faces of young professionals came and went, and the rest of the house was beginning to fill with young students.

I began to realise that the incredible roller coaster of fortune was now at an end and there was no way back – not to who I was before nor to the exhilarating feeling of being on top of the world. There is no doubt that in some ways it had been a success to walk away from the wheel the previous summer, but the terrible affliction was still there. With every subsequent loss, I became more on edge and uncharacteristically angry with those closest to me, those trying to help and support me the most. I was so lucky to be surrounded by supportive and loving family and friends to stop me from completely self-destructing. Something that many other sufferers cannot rely upon.

I quickly lost patience with the hapless accumulators and decided to shorten my odds whilst increasing my bets. Now that I had paid back my debts and started to regain my financial independence, I had something to stake. Despite losing money on some ridiculous accumulators in recent months, my promotion and restraint from the temptations of the material world had allowed me to regenerate some savings.

I placed a three-hundred-pound bet on a single football match. Although it was short odds and a favourite, it was astounding that I could do this to myself after working so hard to take the first few steps to recovery. I can now empathise with those who find themselves plagued by addiction and are pulled back into the void. The demons had simply manifested themselves in another avenue of gambling.

I won this bet and, coupled with my savings over the last few months, I had amassed a total of £2,000. I placed it all on a single bet: the winner of the final in both the UEFA Champions League and the Europa League – Real Madrid and Manchester United respectively. Both were favourites, but I still managed to double my money.

I just could not fight the pull of old glories. I could not let the game rest there. I placed all of the winnings, the £2,800 or so of profit plus the £2,000 stake, on the result of the FA Cup Final. Although it took longer to know the result, in reality this was no different from spinning that little silver ball, and this time my number was up.

15. CASH IN HAND

Tom Petty and the Heartbreakers blasted out "Free Fallin'" live in Hyde Park. I stood on the grass in the warmth of the dreamy July sunshine whilst feeling every drop of a cold beer stoking the flames of the beasts within. And just for a little while, I forgot. I forgot that I'd not only lost all of the money I'd ever had, but somewhere along the line I'd lost myself. I was free falling.

As the gig came to an end and the sun sank behind the stage, I was ready for more. More beer, more excitement, more forgetting! I was there with an old friend but I hadn't seen him since he'd wandered off for a beer about half an hour earlier. I searched around the various free-standing bars and facilities but found no sign of him, and no phone signal. It would have to be the short tube journey back to the hotel and wait there in the hope that we met again with time enough to explore any nearby bars.

It was dark by the time I got to the tube station, but

within ten minutes I was getting on.

"… probably the casino." I overheard the tail end of a conversation between two ladies who were standing across from me in the same tube car. And that last word I struggled to ignore.

"Sorry to interrupt, is there a casino nearby?" I asked, automatically intrigued.

"Yes, apparently there's one close to the next stop."

"It was a great gig, wasn't it?"

The band T-shirts and straw hats were a bit of a giveaway that the two ladies had also been at Hyde Park. They planned to have some final drinks at the casino – one of the few places open and serving at this time of the evening. I swiftly forgot all about my friend and decided this must be divine intervention, the hallowed coincidence to save me from the brink. So, several beers in, it appeared as though I had not fully shaken these delusions.

I thanked the ladies for their directions to the casino, which was a narrow, high-rise type of building over several floors, each of which was ornately decorated. I didn't pay too much attention to the interior and made my way to the nearest cash machine. I extracted fifty pounds, and it came out urgently as a single fifty-pound note. Thinking this was slightly odd, I soon realised it was necessary when I noticed that the even-chance bets on roulette were a fifty-pound minimum. I watched the huddle of punters scrambling around the numbers on the cloth of the roulette table as the croupier flicked a pearly white ball around the wheel. I was back in the game. After all the carnage and devastation, I was here again. Through the lens of several beers, my eye became the roulette wheel. It was all I saw.

I slid my note across the table to the croupier who was about to change my fifty for several chips.

"I'll just have one fifty chip, please." Had I really just said that?

She gave me a quick glance and then slid across a single fifty-pound chip. I fiddled with it for a few minutes and contemplated my next move. She spun the ball once again and it hunted the numbers like a bird of prey. I sat it out and chose not to participate. I wish I hadn't thought about what I might have bet on, as the ball fell into a red number, and I cursed myself for not going for it.

"Any drinks?" A waitress zig-zagged around the tables taking orders.

"Could I have a large whisky, please?"

The thought of a drop of liquid gold to either celebrate or console me was enough encouragement for me to put my chip down. I placed it onto the second half of the table, numbers 19–36. And just like that, the ball landed into number 24, and I'd doubled my money. The whisky arrived just in time to toast the victory.

With a newfound conviction, I placed my two fifty-pound chips on two sets of dozens. I lost. I rose from my seat in disgust and marched to the cashpoint. I felt the whisky coursing through my veins and the warm, fuzzy sensation in my head. I had a sum of four hundred pounds remaining for the month, mostly for food and bills but with the hope that some would be left to recoup some savings for the future. Without any consideration of that, I withdrew half of it, ordered myself another whisky and marched back to the roulette table.

This time I didn't even bother exchanging cash for chips, but stuck a fifty-pound note directly onto red and another on the 1-18 section. I watched the ball in my angry, whisky-infused trance…

… 25, RED.

The croupier took the losing fifty away from the 1–18 section, and matched the winning fifty from the red section with a chip. I switched my bet this time: fifty on black and another on the 19–36 dozen. Nothing ventured, nothing gained.

… 9, RED.

I watched the croupier scrape my losing chip into the tray and the losing note slotted into the cash section. Seeing the note pushed away was a bit of a trigger, and I looked back into my wallet at the remaining notes. I couldn't do it. The combination of the physical act of the transaction and seeing the last few notes I needed to see me through the next month gave me this feeling of complete resignation. I really didn't want to carry this on any longer. I was done with my drink and I was done with this world. I headed straight for the casino exit and I didn't look back. Online and in the flesh, I was done.

16. SLOTS OF CHANGE

The longer term damage of a gambling addiction cannot be underestimated, and it certainly hung on to me for some time. Whilst I had finally turned the corner from the beast of the roulette wheel, I still had a gaping hole inside me. I was moody and irritable, and something felt missing, broken. They were gaps I longed to fill – if gambling wouldn't do it, then they had to be filled by driving some sort of change.

After a couple of years at my shared accommodation, I was struggling to enjoy my blossoming relationship with Jess in the company of carefree, and sometimes careless, students. I had destroyed any hopes of buying a property, so Jess and I would have to rent a place of our own. We found a very small, gardenless cluster house out on the edge of the northern suburbs of Bristol – nothing more was affordable to us, but it was a comfortable place to enjoy a bit of privacy, and in this sense I felt privileged, regardless of how small it was. The distraction of the move soon passed as we settled into our first home together. I spent much time contemplating the last few years and the costly mistakes I'd made to the detriment of myself and those around me. I still had this urge to find meaning from the chaos I'd caused, refusing to accept that it had all just been a dropped stitch in the tapestry. And drastic action would follow.

I applied for a career change, halting my pursuit of professional procurement to join a law enforcement graduate programme. It represented an annual pay cut of over twenty-five percent. Although salary would never be the main factor in my choice of profession, this would be a significant setback in the context of my financial situation following the gambling episodes. I refused to ask myself if it was what I really wanted; I just had to find a new purpose and a new channel for those beasts that were still ravaging my soul deep beneath the surface. The basis of the idea came from my degree in policing and criminology. I was attempting to resurrect a past version of myself. I was like a ghost from a long-dead past life as I embarked on the seemingly endless recruitment process, with several stages, interviews, and assessments. With a head full of doubt being papered over by thoughts of redemption, I packed my bags for a six-week, crash-course training period in London.

As I travelled the dark and dingy tube lines between my accommodation and the training venue, a realisation hit me – I would never be the same person again. I was exhausted from carrying the emotional weight of the mistakes of the last few years. Despite my attempt to get over this with a period of great change and a new challenge, I was still very much at war with the demons of gambling, and more battles lay ahead in the quest to turn the tide.

I had tired of the accumulators and exhausted so many avenues of gambling that all that was really left was the slot machines. More advanced slot machines than ever, with their multiple feature games, impressive graphics, and deceiving formula to rope in gamblers from all corners. So here I was, in temporary, student-esque accommodation, supposedly embarking on a new career and starting a new chapter, but in reality falling on down again under the spell of the house.

After long days of commuting via the tube, being lectured about policing and law enforcement, and undertaking various interactive, role-playing activities, I would retire to the temporary accommodation and spin away the rest of my short but precious evenings on the slot machines.

The speed at which the slot machines swallow money is an unacceptable atrocity. Pay one pound per spin and the screen screams at you with powerful graphics and exclamations to reveal that you have WON! Even for a win line of 20p. That's 80p less than your one-pound stake for a single spin. And you are fully aware of that, yet it is all part of the formula that taps into the competitive, addictive chambers of the mind. These one-pound spins result in rapid spending due to the irregular, infrequent wins, and I found myself spending forty to fifty pounds within the space of about ten minutes. There are very frequent appearances from the bonus symbols, three of which are usually required to open up "special" new games with more significant wins on offer. Two of these symbols appear all too often with the tease of a third before you're let down time and time again. There are also big pots of money appearing permanently on the screen, the infamous jackpots glowing like the mirage of heaven on an endless highway to hell. But the dangling carrot is a classic tactic to keep you spinning away. To keep people betting into oblivion.

Whenever I approached an hour of play, despite a few wins to buy some time, I found myself down by over a hundred pounds. As if I had learned nothing. Although I still had enough restraint to keep to one-pound spins, it was possible to spend ten pounds per spin on a huge variety of games. This was just one more incarnation of the Devil I'd met at the roulette wheel.

I had some small wins over the course of the evenings throughout the training period, but every day I felt on edge. Every day I wanted everything to stop. I didn't want to be there, but these illusions of redemption and a search for purpose got me through it until I could return home to reconsider my situation. I had no choice but to hold it together.

On the final evening, I chose to celebrate my successful completion of the training period with another binge on the slot machines. This time there were no great bonus features to save me from the loss of another one hundred pounds, which I spun away in a matter of minutes. After a long and intensive few weeks on the training programme, I was just as exhausted from the gambling as I was from the period of change I'd forced upon myself.

Upon returning to Bristol, I spent the next few weeks mulling things over and talking it over night after night – I will be forever in debt to Jess for the endless, selfless listening in that period of my self-absorbed nonsense. But it was what I needed to work towards breaking the hold that gambling and its after-effects had on me.

I surrendered to another failure and resigned from the training programme. My new career was over before it really began. I had convinced myself I was looking for redemption, but I still hadn't stopped gambling. After the resignation, I sat down in my small front room, forlorn and defeated. I didn't believe in anything I was doing anymore. I no longer believed in myself. It was time for more change.

I realised I was looking for answers and looking to fill gaps with the wrong ingredients, even if I had good intentions of finding a way out of the gambling world. I'd tried to sidestep into a career I would have to give myself to completely and unquestionably. But you had to be in it for the right reasons. My own psyche was in pieces, and I was deeply troubled about my idea that this new career had been the right choice, to deal with other people's tragedies whilst I wrestled with my own internal conflict. I'd turned my back on a promising career in procurement, which played to my strengths and could still allow me to make some kind of difference in more ways than I gave it credit for. And now I was lost, after trying to plunge myself into another journey before I'd tackled the one I was already on. I knew that I wanted to do something more in the world than just exist for someone else's profit, but my perception of the world, of the institutions of authority, of the human race in general, had all changed. I was someone else.

Suddenly, a "career" and the things we all think are so important, I realised are really not. They are a trade-off. We can trade our time to meet our needs in exchange for the pursuit of passion, and that's what I decided must be done. No longer would I be defined by a "job" or someone else's interpretation of success. The fact of the matter is that we are so hell bent on finding our purpose, filling gaps, and finding answers that we forget how to really enjoy the question. Freedom is really within us.

I had to start being honest with myself: the career change was not the right solution. I would need to think again, and change again. Perpetual change. Over and over. I was exhausted, but I just knew I had to go through this process. A process, that's all it was. I couldn't think any further ahead. I just knew that this attempted career change was one more wrong turn. If you're looking for where to turn, sometimes you should look within instead of around the corner. I was searching for a way to justify all that had gone wrong, but really, I had just been human. I'd been looking for happiness in milestones instead of in the moment. However, before embarking on any mid-career change career change, it was time to mark the end of one era and the beginning of another with one more adventure…

17. MOUNTAIN GOATS IN THE MIST

I've never been one for having swathes of acquaintances, nor have I had any desire to pursue popularity over sincerity. I prefer to keep a small circle of dependable, long-term friends, and, indeed, my closest friends are those from my hometown. But that is not to say that I have shied away from meeting a full spectrum of characters, which was inevitable being raised in the colourful valleys of south Wales.

Today, the gentlemen of the south would be making their way north.

My old friends were fired up for yet another of our classic trips. We had sampled the jazz bars of Europe, walked the coasts and hills of home, crashed and burned many times in the city, but this day would be all about nature. We were headed for the mountains of north Wales, specifically the highest peak in the country: Yr Wyddfa (Mount Snowdon).

It had been about a decade since I had last climbed the mountain, and the last time I'd been there was in the height of summer. We set out amidst the billowing, mid-October winds when I had another of my bright ideas – yes, we would take the most difficult route. The notorious and treacherous Crib Goch ridge, which has claimed the lives of many unfortunate adventurers in the past. I knew all about the fickleness of fortune but aside from the wind, visibility was good, and despite Minty's usual concerns about any of my decisions, we were all looking forward to seeing the wonder of Wales from the very top!

It was really very nourishing to walk out in the expanse, the openness of nature. As we climbed the foothills and scaled the steep, scraggly rocks leading up to the top of the ridge, we spoke of the times we'd shared and those yet to come, and laughed through the wind before sharing a few moments of silence atop the ridge. The wind and the incline were not the only things to take our breaths away, but the morning sun was breaking through a cluster of clouds, shooting beams of light down on the lakes – poetry takes many forms!

Much like the tumultuous twists and turns of a gambler's affair with the house, the power of nature can awaken from a profound silence to tear the world apart in a matter of minutes. And this day would be no exception. It was as if the season had changed before our eyes, and the wind would not relent. The heavens descended and the thickness of the clouds filled the world around us. We could make out the last of the mountain goats in the mist behind us. And suddenly we were the last people on earth. Stranded!

I could hear the sputtering of my hapless

compatriots walking just behind me, in disbelief that they had trusted another of my notorious navigation decisions. But it was far worse than ever before, and we all began to feel uneasy, clinging on to an ever-steepening ridge of jagged rock, surrounded by shale, with no sight of the tourist path in the foothills below and no sign of any other hikers.

"It's going to be dark soon… I've got to get off this mountain!" I heard Minty exclaim.

This was familiar – he was at the back of the pack, ranting about his predicament. And as he said those words, I almost lost my footing. I gasped as the wind tried to push me over the edge. My palms began to tingle as I glanced over the side of the ridge to the sheer drop into the void; I had never been a fan of heights, despite my quests to conquer mountains!

We shuffled sideways across a protruding section of rock and suddenly our fears began to subside. Sunlight beamed through a small break in the cloud cover to reveal a footpath. It felt like the pathway to heaven! We caught our breaths, and light-hearted conversation returned. Despite still being some way off the peak, it felt like we had climbed another kind of mountain and it gave us the spark to continue. Another bad idea.

Nature cannot be underestimated, and it gave us another lesson as we soon became consumed once more by the mist and the promise of the footpath evaporated. We reached another terrifying section of protruding rock and began to question our decision to scale lower down into the shale. We stopped in our tracks and began to contemplate our predicament.

We could hardly hear each other over the billowing gale, and the mist continued to thicken around us. I continued to blank out the horrible thought of ending the adventure on a mountain rescue helicopter – dead or alive! As we sat there, taking some time to consider our next steps, I knew there would be verses and poems born from the ordeal.

I advised the group that I would test the downward slope to see if we could traverse across the very lowest reaches of the shale. I stumbled down and called the others to join me. At last, the gale relented for a moment, and I was able to shuffle onto some walkable terrain. We continued on a slow, careful scramble across the pathless landscape.

The next half an hour or so was very uncomfortable, and it felt as though we were hanging on to the edge of the world. Though, there was some solace in the predicament. Being encompassed by the expanse of nothingness and the power of nature does so much for one's perspective and really makes you contemplate your existence – what really matters?

I had inflicted a cycle of perpetual change onto myself in the last year or so. Throughout that change, I had been writing. That had also been a solace... and release, renewal. It got me through. I wrote and wrote, sometimes out in pockets of beautiful nature, other times of the things I observed on those lonely nights on the tube, or riding a bus to the centre of the city. We can find meditation in the menial. It would sometimes be a few poignant words forming in my head, other times several lines.

In that moment of epiphany, the clouds began to disperse and we could see the main tourist way down below.

The wind and the mist soon turned to heavy rain, but we gave it no regard. We were overjoyed to be back on the beaten track despite being hours behind schedule. And when we finally reached the peak, we felt as though we had conquered the world. Nature is medicine.

We polished off the day with another misguided mishap and took a much longer route back down the mountain, adjacent to the railway. Our heavy legs carried us on to nightfall and took us down to an old guesthouse, now open as a small pub for wayward ramblers. The landlord could not believe we had traversed the ridge in such conditions as he served us all a bottle of Snowdonia Ale. After such a journey, it felt like the golden nectar of heaven!

This day was about perspective. A turning point in my state of mind. We are each but a very small custodian of this living, breathing planet Earth. That is not to say that our journeys mean nothing, but that they are in a state of flux. Time bounds on, mercilessly. And nothing makes you more alive than being on the edge of the world. That was the day I resigned from my quest to right my wrongs or to somehow redeem a past version of myself. All that had been was gone, and it was time for tomorrow…

18. BINGE BETTING

I wish I could tell you that it only took one dose of nature's medicine to complete my full recovery. Unfortunately, whilst the fall into a gambling addiction can be fast-paced and devastating, recovery can be a road which is long and, at times, seemingly insufferable. I had reached a landmark point in my recovery, and now had knowledge and experience that would equip me with the strength to leave the worst of it behind. However, the scars and the gaping holes left by this torrid addiction were long lasting. I was still hankering after something – if not a kind of redemption, then what? Perhaps a foolish desire to have some sort of last laugh. The gambling drug feeds on these desires. Whilst I had tackled the worst of the problem and saved myself from even more tragic loss, I was still not rid of the after-effects, and I wrestled with my job and career choices whilst struggling to moderate my gambling.

I was lucky enough to find myself a route back into my previous profession in procurement, which allowed me to continue with my professional qualifications. I was very grateful to have found a period of stability, but I hadn't returned to this profession as the same person I was when I left it. I continued to suffer with prolonged bouts of guilt and disappointment, and inordinate periods of self-doubt as a result of walking away from the challenge of a new career. I knew there'd be questions about my resignation. There'd be shock and disappointment, and a perception that I was unable to cope. And the truth is, I wasn't able to cope, but the reasons for this were once again buried in the basement. I hadn't realised just how long it would take for me to regain trust in myself, my instincts and my own decision making. But ultimately, this was a necessary process in stepping away from the pursuit of what I thought the world wanted me to be. Now it was time to just simply be. But then came Christmas.

As had been the tradition for the last few years, I parted ways with Jess for the festive period, and we returned to our families for a couple of days. This period of downtime was an opportunity to reflect on the year that had passed and to contemplate the one to come. The feeling of sick emptiness and the yearning to make up for past mistakes were common themes in my gambling episodes, and it seemed that this time of year drew me back to the slot machines with those same feelings.

To a bystander, slot machines probably seem quite baffling. Paying hard-earned money to watch a bunch of mindless reels and symbols spinning around, time after time?! Well, yes, I guess you're right. But when you fully

111

immerse yourself in exactly how they actually work, and you experience the big hits of winning large amounts, it's incredibly surprising how easily you can become gripped by their horrible vice.

They are very formulaic, but not enough to make them overly monotonous or tedious. Aside from the bonus symbols I've mentioned, there are "special features" which don't require any specific outcomes and happen seemingly at random. I believe they are mostly random, but their frequency is what makes things incredibly frustrating. They also very cleverly rope you in with consistent "near misses", and this can be a very powerful psychological trap which convinces you that it's more likely to happen because there have been so many of these near misses. I think you know deep down that this is a fallacy, but it almost creates a cognitive dissonance. You have the devil and the angel at odds with each other in the same brain.

The formula aside, there are occasions where the slots throw out big wins, which are incredibly enticing and tap into chemical reactions in the brain – even though most of the time you've already bet considerable amounts before this actually happens. They are the rush I've mentioned previously, the sense of exhilaration you remember. It's what keeps you coming back. And they know it. They know it all too well.

On Christmas Day, I sickeningly spent three hundred pounds, the remainder of my bank balance for December, in a slot machine trance. I was under the illusion that one pound per spin of the reels would ensure appropriate moderation. But the rate at which gambling companies swallow this money is obscene. Fairness or sympathy has no place in their philosophy. The machines and their formulas are as greedy and unforgiving as the primary stakeholders in these gambling companies – taking huge sums of money at the expense of the most vulnerable. In less than ten minutes, fifty pounds or more can be easily sucked into the black hole of the slots. So, at this rate, you can imagine how quickly the loss moves into triple figures. The longer you play, the more you lose.

I went through a painful period throughout the next year, where I let these binge-betting episodes take hold. It was akin to a move from a daily alcohol dependency to regrettable episodes of binge drinking. As with many gamblers, I felt the huge regret that I was such a hypocrite – bemoaning the ills of capitalism whilst supporting its underbelly with these terrible episodes. The deposit limit tool was always in use to make sure I never let those demons fully take hold again, but I deeply regretted wasting these funds, and if I'd recognised this more fully, I would have set stricter deposit limits. It held back my savings for a mortgage deposit. More to the point, there were so many vulnerable, desperate people in need, and so many great causes that I could have chosen to support with the money I had thrown away. The self-loathing would creep back in from time to time, but I had to keep on going. I knew I was on the right road to complete recovery. The more I engrossed myself in my writing, exercise, work and qualifications, and my close relationships, the less frequent these episodes became.

The less I looked to them for salvation or for a sense of purpose.

The more I fought off the temptation to indulge in episodes of binge betting, the more money I managed to accumulate and put to some positive use. Instead of turning to gambling, I was writing. The creative juices were helping to channel the pent-up energy of the beasts in the basement. I wrote poetry as I rode the buses to and from our small abode to the hustle and bustle of Bristol city centre. I tackled feelings of dislocation and tied them together with words. My clouded lenses seemed to clear, and I was able to enjoy progressing within my profession. Whilst I was long past being defined by a job, a qualification, or a career, it was at least a positive mental stimulant to channel my inner energies in a way which could be enriching as opposed to damaging.

But just as everything seemed to be making sense again, the world ground to a halt.

19. COLD TURKEY

The Covid-19 global pandemic brought everything and everyone to a standstill. Capitalism began to experience a taste of its own poison as the virus spread through the population. Many lives would be lost, and many more changed forever. The world of work transformed beyond all recognition, and it was going to take some time for social isolation to pass and for some kind of normal to return.

My working arrangements during the initial phase of the pandemic were less than ideal, with two of us working in a very small, one-bedroom half-a-house for the whole day and then restricted from any social interaction outside of that chasm in several-month blocks of total lockdown. But I had to keep shaking myself out of self-absorption and reminding myself that I was so much more fortunate than many – I had a roof over my head, warmth, food in the cupboards. Really, I was lucky. I was also lucky to be living in a place where emergency workers, nurses, doctors, and other front-line staff were putting their lives and those of their loved ones at greater risk to keep people safe.

Sadly, that's not the whole story. There were also widespread and abhorrent displays of the selfishness of human nature. Some people completely disregarded the safety of others, and others panic-bought in the early days, buying unnecessary amounts of particular food items or household necessities with a total disregard for those who might go without. "As long as I'm ok." These people have a mindset generated, engineered, and actively encouraged by this self-absorbed, self-involved form of ultra-capitalism. They walk around with a total lack of awareness and a complete sense of self-entitlement. "I am going somewhere to get something, and everyone else should step aside."

This yin and yang of life, both the marvel and the misery of the human race, shaped much of my writing throughout the pandemic. I wrote volumes of poetry and began featuring on local radio, as well as working with some wonderful jazz musicians who were supporting the poetry and spoken word movement with their talents.

All of this positive energy put me far closer to complete recovery, and the gambling episodes seemed to have totally subsided. Even so, I still did not feel quite ready to return to an occasional, and exceptionally small-value flutter on football accumulators or horse racing bets at this stage. For now, I decided to stay away completely. Cold turkey. At least whilst I was riding the waves of the ocean of life, rather than simply staying afloat, or even drowning!

I gained another promotion amidst the pandemic and moved into an area with considerable management duties and a pace of work far exceeding that of the pre-pandemic world. Home and work boundaries became more difficult to set in stone, and despite living in a world of disconnection, some things had never been more connected... in a virtual sense. Meanwhile, owing in some part to my complete avoidance of any potential gambling disasters, Jess and I had managed to save enough money to buy our own house. And this meant a return to Wales after finding a place to call our own just across the border in Monmouthshire. It was nice to be a dweller out on the threshold, as well as being back in my homeland. It felt more in keeping with who I really was – making progress through hard work, not by selling my soul to the demons of capitalism.

Despite all these positive channels and my recovery, my promotion did not quite turn out to be the promised land. I found myself at odds with a hierarchical, authoritarian management, of people who were hyper focused on satisfying their immediate superiors whilst blaming their subjects for any difficulties – it was almost a microcosm of the wider world. I am not one to stand for that sort of leadership, if you can even call it that, and, as a result, found myself in a constant state of conflict. I awoke each morning with a ball of anxiety brewing in the pit of the stomach.

I took positive action. I turned my back on the futile search for solutions through the world of gambling, and instead focused on the right channels. I consistently used the gym and lifted weights at least three times a week, I took walks in nature with our new puppy, and of course wrote poetry. I have never been more certain about the need for, and the benefit of, finding channels for your inner energies and making sure that basement deep down inside you does not explode.

Many months passed, and I seized an opportunity to take up a new position in another department. I knew I could not go on as I was, especially if I was to continue with my recovery into the long term. This was to be another important moment within a period of perpetual change. I knew that there would be far more to come in the journey of life, but I had doubts about whether I was just running away from yet another challenge – one more sidestep when life got too much for me.

A few months into my time in the new department and this self-doubt fizzled into the abyss. I restored faith in myself, my decision making, my instincts, and, of course, my inner voice. All of the persistent change up to this point could easily have been perceived as a naive and restless unhappiness, but I knew this was the latter stage of my full recovery. My confidence and self-belief were regrowing from the ashes of my old self. I was starting to support social and economic improvement projects which were far more in keeping with my core values. I turned my back on gambling, and had begun to find a place where I felt I could express myself, and people who genuinely valued my contributions. I'd found my stone in the earth, and I'd started to etch my mark into it.

20. POET'S CORNER

Poetry. For me, it has really always been there. Yet it has taken me until now to really consider and reflect on that. As a small child, I wrote a poem for my mother as part of a school project, which really moved her. A few years on from that, I had a short poem published in a local newspaper. Although I'd always had quite a natural flair for writing, in my education I was poetically inspired by other subjects.

I was in a history lesson in my first year of secondary school, and our teacher could well have been from a bygone era – he was fast approaching retirement and probably felt he had served more than his fair share in the education system. He wrote with chalk on the board in big white letters: 'KING JOHN.'

"Now!" he exclaimed sternly as the class fell silent in the chill of the winter, with the draft blowing through the rattling windows of the ancient school building. "Can anyone tell me anything about King John?"

"He was a king. And his name was John," I retorted,

without giving it the once-over in my head that I probably should have done!

"Oh! Trying to be funny are we, BOY?! GET OUT!" It was somewhat out of character for the quiet, reserved child that I was under most circumstances, but I was establishing the beginnings of a dry, deadpan sense of humour. I was obviously still developing the knack of knowing my audience. The old history teacher was already disillusioned with his students, and that distasteful one-liner would not have done anything to help matters.

I kept my head down after that, and the lessons progressed to include some Welsh history, specifically the life of Owain Glyndŵr, leader of the Welsh fight for freedom against English rule and oppression in the early 1400s. We studied various parts of his life and were subsequently tasked with writing a poem about it. Hence came another set of verses, which deeply moved the old teacher. I had redeemed my reputation with him, and, from that day on, it also seemed as though there was a little spring in his step. The power of poetry!

I always hoped that striving for an education would be my ticket to better opportunities in life, and that foresight was so important in an environment where I was often surrounded by disillusioned hopelessness, so many taking the path of least resistance, one that really does lead to nowhere. The distractions were easy to obey in the post-industrial mining valleys where colonial extraction had come, had taken, and had left the generations behind. Forgotten.

The poetry fell silent in my adolescence as I faced

the challenges of growing up in a disadvantaged, working-class community. But I do not wish to bemoan my circumstances, for not only did they equip me with a strong, unique, and grounded perspective, but my feelings of privilege came from non-financial sources – I had the gift of a wonderful, loving family.

As I embarked upon adulthood, the poetry came back around once again – because, in one way or another, we all go back to where we belong, don't we? It started with some war memorial poetry prompted by a Remembrance Day event, and later came the desire to pay homage to my late grandmother.

A friend of mine, Daniel Parsons, who was at the time setting out on his journey as an author, recalled my occasional attempt at the art of the verse. He called me up to ask if I would be interested in working with a Cardiff-based publisher wanting to increase their portfolio of poetry. I spoke at length with them about the publishing world, which was all very alien to me. I didn't think a great deal more about it, but I sent in a few pieces of poetry that I had written over the years – they were all very old excerpts as I hadn't really explored my passion for words for quite a while. And just like that, we agreed that a volume would be released at the end of the year… and so it began.

The goal of writing a body of work for a full volume was a further iron in the fire, something else to channel those demons. All of those unwritten poems deep down inside, in the basement, suddenly erupted through my veins and out into the pen. Over the course of the previous year, and in the coming weeks and months, I wrote about all the things I had always really wanted to express, from experiences of working-class Wales to the environment, the human condition, and the search for purpose. I have now written several volumes of poetry, performed readings at art festivals, collaborated with musicians, and, I sincerely hope, stayed true to my inner voice. I found poetry and poetry found me. It has been the making of me.

I have been very fortunate to have a solid foundation of family and friends that so many gamblers do not. Gambling is a vicious cycle of addiction that has been actively encouraged by the industry. A revolution is needed to protect people from themselves, but also to serve as a reminder that no matter how disciplined, how intelligent, sensible, or aware you may think you are, no one is immune to a gambling addiction. I am proof of that. A gambling addiction can be stealthy, voracious, and frighteningly rapid in both its onset and its damaging effects. It can devastate the lives of the afflicted but also of those closest to them. Although my story may be from a comparatively comfortable perspective, given my positive surroundings and network, I hope that it does serve as a reminder that if anyone can be taken by gambling, then the most vulnerable in our society should especially be protected as much as possible from this disgraceful exploitation.

The scars are ingrained, but my perspective on monetary value has returned to some kind of normality, although the odd lapse along the way did often make me question whether or not this would ever be possible again – for many it is certainly not. My work feels as though it is back on track, and I successfully completed my remaining professional procurement qualifications. I slowly regained confidence in my decision making and my instincts. Instead of chasing the butterflies of yesterday, I rediscovered my real passions: health and exercise, walks in nature, environmentalism, Welsh history and the future of our nation, my relationships with my close family and friends, as well as one of my most powerful tools to channel energy… writing. I may have been forced to leave behind my home in search of greater opportunities, but now I can use my voice to tell our story. The forgotten should be heard. And I didn't need drastic changes or momentous checkpoints to get here. Although it can bring its own challenges and tragedies, the pursuit of passion is the only way to maintain belief in yourself. And this is the key to keeping things truly real.

Whilst writing or other creative pursuits may not be a salvation from gambling for other very troubled gamblers or addicts, I found it to be one of many positive channels for life's energy. Taking back your self-control can start with the most (seemingly) insignificant steps forward. Talking and reaching out to the support and networks that are available is the most powerful of first steps, especially for those without the strong foundations that I am lucky enough to have. Nobody should have to fight alone.

The search for purpose and solace is a lifetime pursuit. It doesn't exist in massive milestones or forced periods of change, but in the quiet corners of our undiscovered passions. I firmly believe that happiness comes from within. It is not a destination, nor found in external things such as new or more possessions; it is a state of being and a state of mind.

A glass of fortune, drink of choice,
It's the gambler's time to make his mark.
Spinning the wheels that race through life,
Men of the highest order,
Falling on down with the Devil's bite.

Numbers floating through the air,
Rolling dice without a care,
Marching on to the beat of the drum
All you own is all you have won.

Wrapped in a storm after one last spin,
The house is the one with the final grin.
Look around you,
At all that is left,
All you ever needed,
Not a glass of fortune, guilty as sin,
Breaking even feels like a win.

No more tricks up the sleeve,
Time to stop, to breathe.
Folding the hand before the lonely walk home,
The gambling man has a long way to go.
Stack the odds and hang the head,
The headstone waits for the name,
Of the lucky man that played one more game.

Secrets in the head, the demon is unleashed.

Walking free and out of the fold,
If you drink a glass of fortune,
Beware,
And don't make it too bold.

Printed in Great Britain
by Amazon